THE CHANGING FACE OF
LEEDS

THE CHANGING FACE OF
LEEDS

BRIAN GODWARD

SUTTON PUBLISHING

Sutton Publishing Limited
Phoenix Mill · Thrupp · Stroud
Gloucestershire · GL5 2BU

First published 2004

Title page photograph: Old and new contrast
high above City Square.

British Library Cataloguing in Publication Data
A catalogue record for this book is available from the
British Library.

ISBN 0-7509-3413-1

Typeset in 10.5/13.5 Photina.
Typesetting and origination by
Sutton Publishing Limited.
Printed and bound in England by
J.H. Haynes & Co. Ltd, Sparkford.

BRIAN GODWARD was a Leeds man through and through. He was born in Harehills, Leeds, in 1932 and was educated at the City of Leeds School. He then studied for a Diploma in Architecture at Leeds College of Art. He subsequently worked as an architect for Harrogate Hospital Board, the Yorkshire Electricity Board and in the Planning Departments of Bradford and Leeds City Councils. The big change in his life came in the late 1960s when he became a lecturer in architecture at Leeds Polytechnic. Brian joined the Leeds Civic Trust in 1971 and in the same year he became a member of Trust Council, and by the following year he was listed as a member of the Planning Development and Preservation Committee. By 1973 he had added to his portfolio the chairmanship of the Waterways Committee. Though Brian took early retirement from the Polytechnic, he was thrilled soon to be back at work as a Conservation Officer for Harrogate Borough Council.

He was an excellent researcher, narrator and photographer and was dedicated to perfection in the illustration and production of both his own, and numerous other, publications. He was a quiet, gentle, soft-spoken man whose knowledge and enthusiasm touched all. This last publication was completed just before his death.

CONTENTS

PREFACE

When we build, let us think we build forever.
John Ruskin, *Seven Lamps of Architecture*, 1847

Ruskin, the eminent critic and philosopher on art, architecture, social reform and environmental issues, would have been alarmed could he have seen much of today's building. In our fast-changing world, 'permanence' is not usually a critical requirement, at least beyond a modest lifespan. 'Monuments' are not called for; speed of construction, flexibility and cost are all-important. Our new factory estates and supermarkets are usually simple 'sheds'. On the question of change I can offer a personal example. Some forty years ago I designed a large building for a public utility to house its first generation of computers. Today only

about a tenth of the original floor area is needed to carry out the same functions using state-of-the-art electronics. So much for forward planning, out with the crystal ball!

Fortunately our forebears usually 'built to last' and we have ample evidence of their considerable efforts. Heritage (to use an overworked word) is not just that which is great, grand or ancient. A look at most pre-1940 guide books reveals a concentration on the great cathedrals, historic castles and stately houses, every corner described in great detail (and in small print!). Of course such structures are important, but so are the buildings of the 'ordinary' men and women of the past. The Board schools, mills, pubs, cinemas, swimming baths – possibly even a Victorian workhouse – were part and parcel of working-class life, for better or worse. We now have a wider

view of what constitutes our heritage. Architecture is important but so are the social and economic conditions that gave rise to these buildings at that particular time. That august body, the National Trust, recognises the wider interpretation of heritage. You can now visit such diverse properties as a Victorian workhouse, the modernised home of an eminent twentieth-century architect and the 1950s council house of Sir Paul McCartney's family.

The buildings included in my review are my own personal choice, hopefully illustrating (albeit briefly) some one thousand years of historic and architectural development in Leeds and district. However, all these buildings, structures and other features have been 'listed'. This simply means that they have been recognised by the government as important in the rich pattern of our history, and so should be preserved and protected for future generations. There is more about listing in the introduction.

I hope that you enjoy this little book. It may bring back personal, hopefully happy, memories. You might find it useful as a reference source and, though I have had to be brief, I have included a bibliography listing some very good informative publications. Leeds and its surrounding towns, villages and countryside have a long and interesting history. Go see for yourself. You will be surprised by some quite bizarre features, puzzled by others, but impressed by the quality of some magnificent architecture.

A morning view towards the city from Meanwood Valley.

Old and new contrast high above City Square.

Inner-city area in transition: Woodhouse and the Lower Meanwood Valley.

Back-to-back houses in Woodhouse typical of many built over a century ago.

Open rural landscape near Harewood with the River Wharfe just beyond the horizon. This is a listed former farmhouse in local stone and slate.

Thorp Arch Village (near Boston Spa) in springtime. The village is one of many conservation areas within the Leeds district.

A high-level city vista looking east along
The Headrow.

The Riverside east of Crown Point Bridge at Leeds
Dam. New apartments look across to the Royal
Armouries.

Modern shopping: the White Rose Centre in
south-west Leeds.

The city is famed for its many parks and open
spaces, which occupy a high proportion of its land
area. This one is Golden Acre Park in the north-
west of the district.

One of the attractive market towns in the district.
This is Wetherby on a Thursday with shoppers
around the Town Hall.

This is Bramham Park, set in magnificent
eighteenth-century parkland in the north-east of
the district.

Vernacular buildings in the west of the district. Built using sandstones and gritstones, these domestic structures are typical of the locality. Clockwise from top left: The Nunnery, Arthington Lane; Cottages, Main Street, Shadwell; Former Grammar School, Clapgate Otley; High Farm Public House, Farrar Lane.

Introduction: The Many Faces of Leeds

VERNACULAR – 'of one's country, indigenous, not of foreign origin or of learned foundation.' (*Oxford English Dictionary*)

A SENSE OF PLACE

Generally, prior to the nineteenth century and the introduction of canals and railways, building was very much a local craft and architects as we know them today were not involved with the 'ordinary' humble cottages and farms. Britain is noted for its remarkable diversity of vernacular architecture which adds distinctive colour and texture to early settlements, so giving that 'sense of place' lacking in today's modern developments.

Two basic factors applied. First there was the necessary use of locally found building materials. Secondly, the form of buildings was governed by climatic conditions and the degree of exposure. These factors tend to 'root' older buildings to their immediate landscape, so that they merge naturally with the local scene.

Limestone buildings in the east of the district. Town Hill in Bramham Village, which was once on the Great North Road.

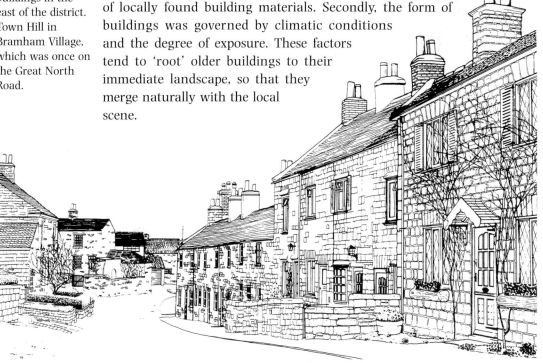

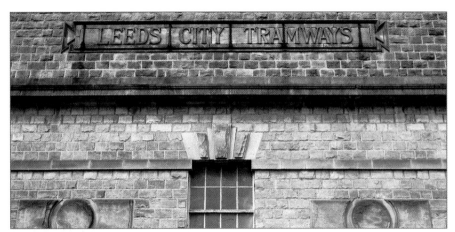

Gritstones and sandstone were quarried in the north and west of the district. Here is the former Leeds City Tramways Depot at White Cross, Guiseley.

Magnesian limestone was quarried in the east of the district. Here we see the Wesleyan chapel at Wetherby.

Brick clays and terracotta – these materials were found in east and south Leeds, together with coal. This photograph shows the former Baptist church, Meanwood Road, Leeds, which is now in commercial use.

Early local village buildings in the Leeds district share these characteristics. The area, from a geological viewpoint, is on the northern edge of the Yorkshire coalfield with coal measures underlying much of the southern and central parts of Leeds. To the west and north is a large area of millstone grit, this and the coal measures yielding sandstones ranging from coarse to fine grain. To the north and east along the A1 (the former Great North Road) and the district boundary is found magnesian limestone, while in the south and east of the area lie ample deposits of brick earths.

West of Leeds, Bradford is very much a 'buff' sandstone city; very little red brick can be seen. Outer Leeds 'villages' such as Guiseley, Yeadon, Pudsey and Stanningley merge visually with Bradford's suburbs in this use of sandstone, much of it originally quarried in the Aire Valley. The nature of the material gave an overall unity of stone colour to some streets, with walls, roof slates, paving flags and road setts (sometimes called 'cobbles') of a similar material. In contrast, where Leeds borders the Plain of York, the older settlements are of quite a different colour. Soft, creamy-white magnesian limestone was used, the towns and villages of Wetherby, Bramham, Boston Spa, Aberford and Ledsham being typical of this character, which is also found in Tadcaster and York. Unlike the sandstone villages in the west of the district, the A1 corridor settlements were not affected by nineteenth-century industrial pollution and so retain a fresh, clean appearance.

The third major traditional material is that of brick, produced by moulding clay from local pits. Bricks were readily available in south and east Leeds and the rapid expansion of the area during the nineteenth century was largely carried out in red brick, particularly that of the many terraces of housing. Much of this remains today, the 'bye-law' streets of Harehills, Hyde Park, Burley and Kirkstall still providing accommodation for many people. At Burmantofts, east Leeds, both fine-quality clay and coal deposits were extracted from the same shafts. High-quality terracotta, faience and glazed ceramics were produced, many of which can be seen on Leeds buildings, as well as being exported worldwide.

The introduction of Conservation Area legislation in 1967 has protected many of the older and traditional Leeds 'villages' from unwanted and unsympathetic changes. This is perhaps more important in urban examples, now engulfed by suburbia. Some of these pre-date the Norman Conquest, and there are eighteenth-century cottages in villages such as Headingley, Chapel Allerton, Armley and Bramley setting standards for the new infill housing which respects layout, design and above all the use of appropriate materials.

LOOKING AFTER THE PAST

In this short review of the architecture of the Leeds Metropolitan District I have made a personal selection of those listed buildings that I consider to have been important in the growth and development of this great city and its hinterland. Less than 1 per cent of those listed are included in this study. But, first, what does listing mean and what does it entail?

'Listing' describes briefly the legal process by which buildings and other features are protected, so conserving the best of the past for future generations. This leads to their inclusion in the statutory 'lists of buildings of special architectural or historic interest', those for Leeds being available for reference in the local history library and some branch libraries. The expertise of the staff of English Heritage is used to advise government on which buildings merit inclusion in these lists, supported by local councils, amenity and historical groups and members of the public. Local interest, knowledge and commitment have saved many important buildings from demolition. Once a building has been listed, consent must be received from the local council (occasionally English Heritage) prior to any work that would affect its special character, or, in very rare cases, its demolition.

Nationally, less than 4 per cent of buildings are listed, these being carefully selected to possess the qualities that will be appreciated and enjoyed by future generations. Historic buildings are a precious and finite asset, reminding us of the ways of life of our predecessors. These buildings left to us by previous generations give us a sense of time and place, enriching the quality of our surroundings.

The lists include not only buildings but also other features. In the Leeds district over 3,300 items are listed, including several bridges, many monuments and memorials, together with minor features such as gas lamps, mileposts, a post box and one horse trough. There are also some unusual structures, including a First World War aircraft hangar, privies, remains of a zoo, a sham castle folly and a 1930s petrol station now in use as a civic fountain. Few buildings of the twentieth century are listed in Leeds, the nineteenth century providing a much greater number echoing the massive expansion of the city during the Industrial Revolution.

Listing of a building does not mean that it is available for public access. Some civic buildings are obviously in public use and may be entered; other important buildings may be visited on payment of an admission charge. Most of those included in this review can be seen from the public highway. However, in all cases the privacy of the owners or occupiers should be respected.

1   Early Beginnings

This chapter covers the period AD 900 to about AD 1680, encompassing the end of medieval Saxon rule and the culmination of the Gothic era. Saxon churches are the oldest surviving English buildings, but none is intact as a complete example of the period. However, at Bardsey one can see a fine tower of the time, and a handful of local churches have evidence of Saxon origins although all have been substantially altered. The people were uneducated and primitive and much of their building work was on a small scale and crude in nature, but this was to change after 1066.

The Normans introduced a whole new social, economic and organisational regime. There was a massive development in churches and monasteries; in Leeds the Cistercian Kirkstall Abbey is one of many in the county. Men were strongly influenced by a deep religious fervour, life was dangerous and insecure and many castles were built in Yorkshire, though in the district only one survives (above ground) at Harewood, overlooking the Wharfe valley. On a positive note, the invaders introduced superior technical skills in building with stone. Initially they used thick walls with small windows and large round columns supporting semi-circular arches. Later through the centuries their successors created much higher and lighter structures with huge windows and delicate stone tracery. Our great cathedrals are witness to some magnificent examples of the skills of generations of craftsmen in stone, timber and glass.

The great majority of buildings of the period, the ordinary houses, were of timber, mud and thatch. Only a few fragments remain today of such dwellings; time, weather and fire have taken their toll. Towards the end of this period the use of brick became popular for important buildings, largely because of Italian and Dutch influences. In the Jacobean period Templenewsam House was founded. In style it is very different from the early Gothic; a step towards the Classical era is evident, with the roofs masked by decorated parapets above a 'U'-shaped plan around a courtyard.

FROM SAXON TIMES TO THE COMMONWEALTH

Little is known about the history of Leeds and its hinterland prior to the Norman Conquest and the Domesday records of 1086. The Romans certainly occupied the area, there being evidence in the materials and artefacts unearthed at Adel and in isolated locations in and around the present city centre. Historians suggest there might have been a Roman (or

Church of All Hallows, Bardsey,
Church Lane.

Saxon?) fort at Quarry Hill. However, extensive excavations for buildings during the town's rapid expansion during later centuries is likely to have destroyed any traces of an actual Roman settlement.

The earliest architectural evidence that can be viewed is from the Anglo-Saxon period in the ninth or tenth century. The Anglian cross inside Leeds Parish Church dates from about AD 925. Its design shows Viking and Scandinavian influences, beautifully carved with figures and knot work.

There are some important Saxon churches in the district. Very few Saxon churches remain today in their original form; being very small, mos have been altered and enlarged over the years. The characteristic feature primitive Saxon building work is that of its crudeness and lack refinement, with a few exceptions. All Hallows, Bardsey, has a simple

Church of All Saints, Ledsham, Claypit Lane.

unbuttressed tower with two tiny twin-arched openings with central balusters punched through massive stone walls. At Ledsham, All Saints has a tower whose lower part is of Saxon origin in crude stone rubble walling. However, the doorway in the south face is of great interest. A semi-circular arch is surrounded by a projecting band carved with vine scrolls and rosettes. Apart from the towers both churches have evidence in their interiors of Saxon origins, the hallmark of which is that of the tiny spaces created.

The Norman invasion was to bring about enormous changes in the social order and, in turn, the need for more buildings with more advanced construction techniques than those employed by the Anglo-Saxons. The most significant change was the founding of the monasteries. It is hard to believe today that Kirkstall Abbey was once in a quiet and remote wooded valley rather like the setting of Fountains. Cistercian monks from the latter

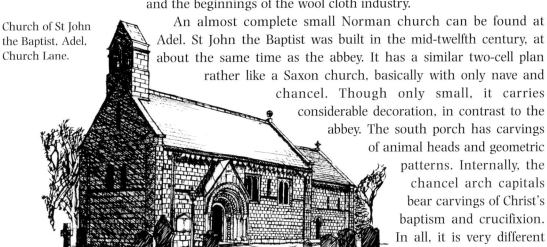

Kirkstall Abbey,
Abbey Road.

founded Kirkstall in 1152, completing the settlement in about thirty years. They followed a similar pattern to Fountains, adopting the strict rules of the Order in their building work, so the abbey structure is rather austere with little decoration. The buildings are in a local millstone grit with typical round arched Norman windows and doors. Changes came later, introducing the pointed Gothic arch, and the great tower was increased in height early in the sixteenth century, just prior to the Dissolution. The abbey was to have considerable influence on the development of the area, with the founding of sheep farming, outlying granges, a forge just up-river and the beginnings of the wool cloth industry.

Church of St John
the Baptist, Adel,
Church Lane.

An almost complete small Norman church can be found at Adel. St John the Baptist was built in the mid-twelfth century, at about the same time as the abbey. It has a similar two-cell plan rather like a Saxon church, basically with only nave and chancel. Though only small, it carries considerable decoration, in contrast to the abbey. The south porch has carvings of animal heads and geometric patterns. Internally, the chancel arch capitals bear carvings of Christ's baptism and crucifixion. In all, it is very different from the plain austerity of the abbey.

HISTORIC &
PICTURESQUE
LEEDS

The unusally
beautiful
SOUTH PORCH
ADEL CHURCH

The ornate
sculptured
pediment &
five receding
arches are
notable examples
of Norman work

The bronze RING of REFUGE on
the oaken door is one of the
very few relics now remaining
in England of days when the
Church provided sanctuary for
witing & unwitting criminals. It
is a link with one of the oldest
customs in the world for it was in
operation 14 Centuries B.C. & 15 after.

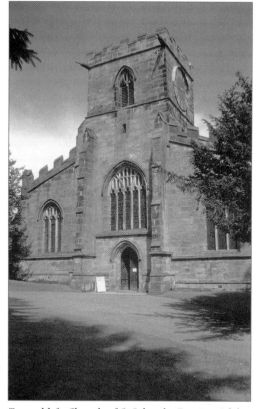

Top and left: Church of St John the Baptist, Adel,
Church Lane.
Above: Church of All Saints, Harewood, Church
Lane.

Other significant parish churches include St Mary's, Whitkirk, and All Saints, Harewood. The former has medieval origins, probably eleventh century, but is now substantially of the fifteenth century. The tower is distinctive, with corner pinnacles, corbelled parapet and a central spire at the west end of a low wide body in a Perpendicular style. All Saints is also fifteenth-century Perpendicular and has a very long nave and chancel. Within are six medieval monuments in alabaster, recumbent couples on tomb-chests dating from 1419–1510, restored 1979–81. It is now in the care of the Redundant Churches Fund.

The oldest surviving major country house or mansion is that of Ledston Hall, which has thirteenth-century origins from when it was a grange of Pontefract Priory, whose monks built a chapel which is now part of the hall undercroft. Outwardly the hall appears to be of the mid-seventeenth century, largely Elizabethan or Jacobean in style, with the outer walls having either simple triangular or more ornate Dutch gables. The corners of the hall are marked with narrow towers rising above the general roofline and capped with shallow ogee roofs. This is a very impressive building in limestone set within extensive grounds. It is not open to the public.

Ledston Hall, Hall Lane.

Templenewsam House, Templenewsam Park.

The other major country house of this period is that of Templenewsam in east Leeds. With origins in the late fifteenth century, it was acquired by Sir Arthur Ingram in 1622, after which it was remodelled as seen today. Many changes have been made to the interior since then and the house was bought by the City of Leeds in 1922. It is now in use as a museum. Architecturally, Templenewsam is in a traditional Elizabethan or Jacobean style in red brick with stone dressings. The roof is concealed behind a balustraded open parapet, and within the courtyard the latter feature carries an inscription in large letters on the theme of Glory to God and the King. 'Capability' Brown was commissioned to landscape the 900-acre parkland in 1762 and his work here is thought to be among the best of his many contracts.

Very few minor secular buildings have survived from this early period, primarily because most were of timber construction. In south Leeds, Stank Hall has a fine aisled barn, the timber structure dated mid- to late fifteenth century. The remains of the manor house of the de Rome family at Cad Beeston include sections of the timber-framed wall from the early fifteenth century. In Oulton can be seen The Nookin, a small house with timberwork set above a masonry base. Finally, off Lower Briggate in Leeds can be found the remaining fragments of the only surviving 'three-decker' in the city centre. This dates from the early seventeenth century but has been much altered throughout its life.

Above: Timber-framed 'three-decker house', 2 Lambert's Yard, Briggate; *below:* Manor House, Cad Beeston, Temple Crescent.

Above: Stank Hall Barn, Dewsbury Road. *Below:* The Nookin, 48 Leeds Road, Oulton.

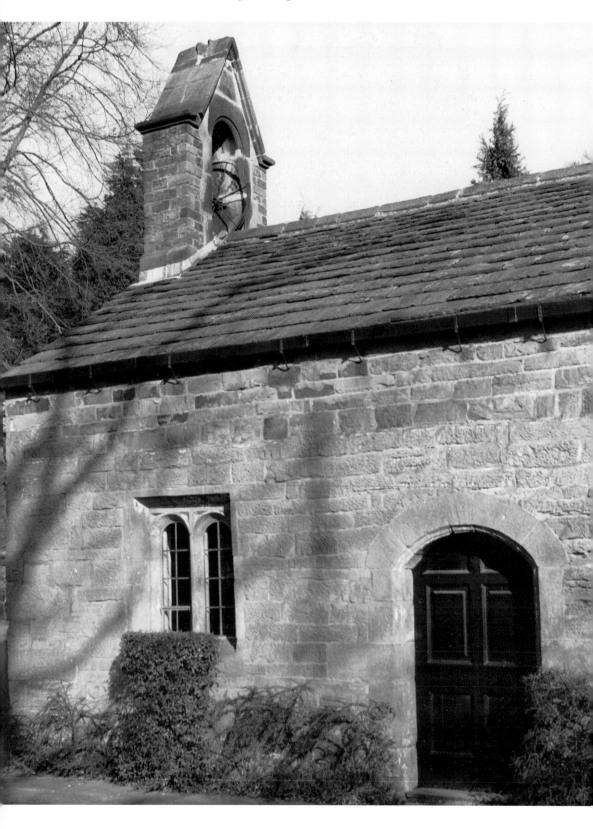

Church of St John the Evangelist, Mark Lane and New Briggate.

Two nationally important places of worship were built within less than twenty years of each other in the first half of the seventeenth century, St John the Evangelist in New Briggate, Leeds, and the Bramhope Puritan chapel. In architectural terms they present strong contrasts, reflecting the faiths and beliefs of their worshippers. They were founded during the turbulent times before the English Civil War and during Oliver Cromwell's Commonwealth.

The chapel was built in 1649 and is said to be one of only two such founded during the Commonwealth and so is of national importance. A very plain and simple stone structure with small mullioned windows, it is without architectural decoration. Founded by Richard Dyneley, the chapel has box pews and a three-decker pulpit.

Opposite: Puritan chapel, Bramhope, Otley Road.

By contrast, St John's, from 1634, looks back to the Perpendicular Gothic of the fifteenth century, with battlements and square-headed windows. Founded by John Harrison, a noted Leeds merchant, it has an

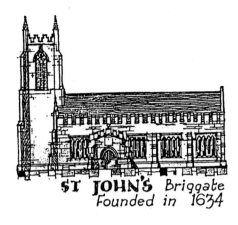

The Church of St John the Evangelist, Mark Lane and New Briggate.

unusual plan form, with twin naves of equal width and a central arcade of stone columns carrying king post roof trusses. The interior is magnificent, with contemporary fittings and furnishings, screen and pulpit, benches and Royal Arms, all from the period. Very few churches were built in the seventeenth century, so St John's is thus of national significance, particularly since its interior is very largely intact, rescued from the attentions of the nineteenth-century 'improvers'. It is now in the care of the Churches Conservation Trust.

2 Down your Way

The Leeds townscape is home to many objects that we walk past without noticing or simply take for granted. They cannot be described as buildings, but all have a function, many well designed and having an historical significance. Today we describe them collectively as street furniture. The older examples give a fascinating insight into life in more leisurely days prior to the coming of the motor car. The tiny stone milepost outside Bramhope church tells us in letters and figures 1 inch high that it is 8.1 (eight miles one furlong) to Leeds Bridge. It was very easily seen as you walked or rode past in yesteryear, but today traffic passes by at 40 mph!

Sadly many historic features such as road signs, horse drinking troughs and bollards have disappeared, victims of highway widening and 'improvements'. Hundreds of the troughs have gone, together with their users. However, you can see one on Otley Road, a basic cast-iron model no doubt produced by the thousand in Asquith's Foundry.

Bramhope, Milepost, Otley Road. Thought to be from the early nineteenth century, this is one of several that can be found along this historic route. Guide post, Wike Ridge Lane/ Wigton Lane junction. A simple iron plaque mounted on to a small pillar. A hand with only four digits points the way. Note the interesting spelling.

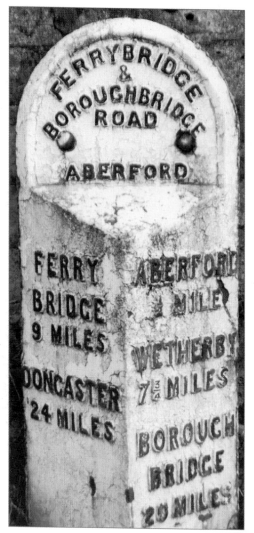

Two roadside features in iron. *Left:* Mileposts, former Great North Road, Aberford. This one is typical of several along this former coaching highway, cast in iron to a standard pattern. *Above:* Horse trough, Otley Road (near St Chads Drive).

One of the finest mileposts stands outside Kirkstall Forge, an elegant obelisk in rusticated stone. An iron plaque proclaims that it lies 'to London 200 miles S' and 'to Edinburg 200 miles N'. Along the Great North Road through Wetherby and Aberford a standard pattern was adopted, with faces pointing to either Ferrybridge or Boroughbridge.

A combination of civic pride and an emerging social conscience which burgeoned in the Victorian era found its physical expression in many unusual ways. Foundries turned out iron products in their thousands, many of them serving to improve the quality of communal life: drinking fountains, benches, street lighting and gas lamps, bollards and the humble foot scraper! In Leeds the Hope Foundry in Mabgate was the source of many street features still with us today.

Opposite:
Milepost, Abbey Road. Dated 1829, this fine obelisk is the o... one of its type i... the Leeds distri...

SCARCROFT TOLL BAR

THIS BUILDING WAS OCCUPIED BY THE TOLL BAR COLLECTOR
AFTER THE CONSTRUCTION OF THE LEEDS/WETHERBY ROAD IN
1826. TOLLS HAD TO BE PAID ON ALL HORSE-DRAWN VEHICLES
AND ANIMALS TO COVER THE COST OF MAINTAINING THE ROAD.
IN 1876 THE TOLL SYSTEM LAPSED AND THE TOLL GATES WERE
REMOVED. IN 1985 THE SCARCROFT PARISH COUNCIL ASSISTED
IN THE REPAIR OF THE BUILDING TO PRESERVE IT.

Scarcroft Toll Bar House, Thorner Lane. Built in 1826 for the Leeds Wetherby Turnpike Road, it is one of several that remain throughout West Yorkshire.

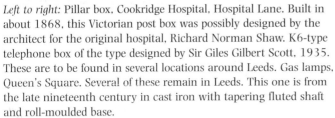

Left to right: Pillar box, Cookridge Hospital, Hospital Lane. Built in about 1868, this Victorian post box was possibly designed by the architect for the original hospital, Richard Norman Shaw. K6-type telephone box of the type designed by Sir Giles Gilbert Scott, 1935. These are to be found in several locations around Leeds. Gas lamps, Queen's Square. Several of these remain in Leeds. This one is from the late nineteenth century in cast iron with tapering fluted shaft and roll-moulded base.

One of the more recent of townscape features is that of the famous K6 Telephone Kiosk designed by the eminent architect Sir Giles Gilbert Scott in 1935. Leeds has several of these, all of which were listed some twenty years ago in a national programme. Six kiosks are to be seen in City Square by the General Post Office and others individually add colour to village conservation areas around the district.

3   An Age of Elegance

The Renaissance in the arts and culture that spread through Europe in the seventeenth and eighteenth centuries was based on studies of Greek and Roman civilisations of over a thousand years before. Intellect and knowledge of the architecture of the period were all-important, with many English noblemen and architects making study tours 'finishing' their education in classical principles.

The Royal Georges reigned during most of this period, so the term 'Georgian' is often used to describe the type of buildings in Park Square and Boston Spa. A growing middle class could now enjoy an elegant comfortable home, benefiting from the rapidly increasing wealth of the country and a social order offering a secure future. Industry was on a relatively small-scale domestic basis, the wool cloth trade being very important economically.

Harewood House.

Brick was now widely employed for most buildings, so houses in a durable material were now possible for most of the people. A high degree of craftsmanship is evident, but it is in the designs based on the principles of Classical proportions that such architecture is so distinctive and typically British.

Later in the period the wealth of the country was concentrated into fewer hands. These men owned huge country estates and were incredibly rich, building magnificent houses within enclosed parklands on a grand scale. Harewood House and Bramham Park are major examples locally. One of the consequences of this was to create considerable change in the countryside economy. The enclosure of much common land and smallholdings that were farmed by the ordinary man deprived many of their livelihood. Most had to move into the towns to find work. The process of rural depopulation had started and by the end of the eighteenth century Britain was to witness massive social and economic upheaval. The Industrial Revolution began in earnest.

IDEAS FROM EUROPE

The Renaissance (or rebirth) of interest in the revival of the art and architecture of Ancient Rome came about in Italy from the early fifteenth century to the sixteenth century. A thousand years had elapsed since the civilisation of Imperial Rome had reached its zenith only to be lost in the chaos of the Dark Ages. It was an architecture of great refinement, with

Austhorpe Hall, Austhorpe Lane, Crossgates (1694).

advanced building and engineering techniques. The culture was based to a large extent on that of Ancient Greece, which Rome had colonised.

The movement took over a century to reach northern Europe, and England in particular. There were few examples until the early seventeenth century. Inigo Jones had studied the exact rules of Classical proportion formulated by Italian Andrea Palladio and was the first Englishman to build according to these rules. The Queen's House at Greenwich (1616) was of revolutionary design and very un-English in character. Jones was to influence later architects, including Christopher Wren, who used the basic principles of Classical design.

Austhorpe Hall, in east Leeds, is probably the oldest surviving building in the area where Classical principles are clearly evident. Built in 1694, it has a hipped roof and symmetrical façade arrangement with a central one-bay pediment. This style was quite different from the local vernacular of the time, the hall being faced with red brick with contrasting quoins of stone.

John Cossins's plan of Leeds, 1725.

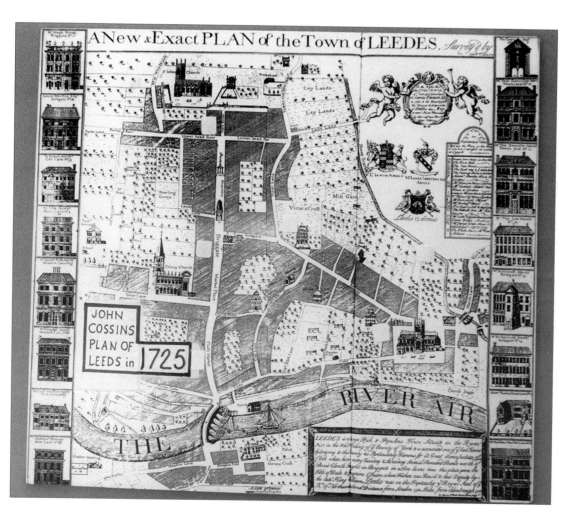

Top left: Former Wool Merchants House, 165–9 Lower Briggate.
Top right: Queens' Court, behind 165–9 Lower Briggate.

The Mustard Pot public house, 20 Stainbeck Lane, Chapel Allerton.

Several similar houses were built in Leeds town centre at about the same time as Austhorpe Hall. They were for the merchants trading in wool cloth, the major reason for the increasing wealth and prosperity of the town. John Cossins's Plan of 1725 has drawings indicating that many of these were very impressive in a Classical style, with some of them three storeys in height. However, all those on the plan have been lost to later developments.

One survivor from this period can be found in Lower Briggate. The house has an extensive and impressive frontage to the former Cloth Market, its central two bays projecting between stone quoins. Behind lies Queens' Court, on an original thirteenth-century burgage plot, with other houses, workshops and warehouses in connection with the early eighteenth-century wool trade. Similar houses are to be found in what are now Leeds suburbs: in Chapel Allerton, the former Clough House (now a public house), and in Halton, Dial House, 1755. Both are in brick stone with stone dressings, the latter with four Venetian-style windows and pedimented door surround.

Dial House, Chapel Street, Halton.

Above: Third White Cloth Hall, Crown Street (1775–6).
Left: Former Assembly Rooms, Crown Street.

The wool cloth trade was booming during the early eighteenth century and business became too large for the open Cloth Market (now Lower Briggate), so a series of Cloth Halls were built. The Third White Cloth Hall, 1775–6, was originally a huge courtyard surrounded by single-storey buildings, within which trading took place until 1865 when the railway viaduct sliced through the area. Only a small fragment remains today, the gatehouse wing with arched entrance and bell cupola. The adjacent Assembly Rooms were erected over the north-east wing of the Cloth Hall and were the centre of Georgian Leeds's elegant social life. Here, in a

Former canal
warehouse,
27 Canal Wharf
(1777).

magnificent upper suite of reception rooms, were held grand balls, concerts
and gaming sessions. The ground floor of the building was in use by the
wool traders, with an arcaded frontage opening on to the courtyard. The
building has an impressive long façade, with a series of recessed arches and
a large central Venetian window rising through the upper two floors.

The century was to see the opening of two economically important
transportation routes. The Aire and Calder Navigation was opened in 1700
and the Leeds and Liverpool Canal was started in 1770. These eventually
reached seaports from which local products could be exported, further
enhancing the growing prosperity of the town. A massive stone warehouse
was built at the eastern end of the latter canal, a robust structure within
which barges could be loaded and unloaded internally from a water dock.
It is an early example of the use of cast-iron columns and beams in
conjunction with masonry arched infill floors.

The preachings of Charles Wesley and others fostered the growth of
Nonconformity in the area and many chapels were founded, a major
Georgian example being at Mill Hill, City Square, Leeds (now replaced by
the nineteenth-century Gothic Revival building). Most were of simple
design, austere with little architectural decoration. Many were double

storey in height with upper galleries. The Methodist Centre in Chapel Allerton is typical of many chapels in the Leeds district, though altered internally.

Perhaps the most important eighteenth-century church in Leeds is that of Holy Trinity, Boar Lane. This provided an elegant place of worship for the wealthy merchants of the town. Completed in 1726, it was designed in a Palladian style by William Etty. The tower is a later addition of 1841, replacing an original spire, and is in the style favoured by Wren and Gibbs.

Towards the end of the eighteenth century the quality of building materials and techniques improved considerably. This is very apparent in the Georgian terraces in the centre of Leeds, in Boston Spa and in other towns and villages locally. In Leeds the brickwork detailing and joinery of the doors and sash windows in the Parks Estate is characterised by its great refinement. The town expanded westwards late in the eighteenth century

Methodist Centre, Town Street, Chapel Allerton (1794).

Holy Trinity Church, Boar Lane (1721–6).

and the Wilson family developed the Square and a series of streets with fine terraces of elegant brick houses. Park Square is most attractive and the whole estate displays the beginning of conscious town planning. Unlike Bath or Edinburgh, there are no grand or unified façades, rather a series of individual houses whose well-mannered frontages conform to established building lines, respecting height and materials. Unity is also provided by the general proportions of the houses and their sash windows. Individuality and variety are apparent in the designs of the door porticos, casings and

Park Square, Park Square North (1788–1810).

The Georgian style. *Left:* A pair of 'semis' in Park Square in brick. *Right:* Elegant terrace in Boston Spa, 215–19 High Street. It was built about 1800 in ashlar magnesian limestone.

fanlights. To the gentlemen of the day there was only one right way to build – not to conform would be in bad taste, almost bad manners. It certainly produced some fine architecture.

This period was witness to the phenomenal development and growth of the great country estates and the age of Classicism in houses and their landscaped parklands. During the late seventeenth and eighteenth centuries Italy and Greece became the 'Mecca' for English noblemen and architects who undertook the 'Grand Tour'. They were keen to study ideas that could be adapted for use on their own personal estates. They found considerable inspiration among the architectural glories of these ancient civilisations, their legacy the magnificent houses and landscapes that we enjoy today. We are fortunate to have many fine examples in the Leeds area, several of which may be visited by the public.

Denison Hall, Hanover Square (1786), designed by William Lindley (a pupil of John Carr) for J.W. Denison. It is now subdivided into apartments.

Cookridge Hall, Cookridge Lane (1754). It is now part of a sports and leisure complex.

Perhaps the finest country house in the district is that at Harewood, home of the Lascelles family for over three centuries and of national importance and significance. In addition to the house, the estate is notable for its other features such as the stables, model farm and village, magnificent parkland and terraces, medieval castle and church. Edwin Lascelles was over forty when he embarked on the ambitious plans for Harewood.

Above: Harewood House, main gateway (1802–4). By Humphrey Repton. *Below:* Harewood Village, The Avenue, Harewood (mid- to late eighteenth century), a model village by John Carr of York.

Opposite, above: Harewood House, South Front, Harewood Park, Harrogate Road. Sir Charles Barry after John Carr and Robert Adam. *Opposite, bottom:* The South Terrace and parkland. The terrace was designed by Sir Charles Barry for Louisa, Lady Harewood in 1848, and the park was designed by 'Capability' Brown in 1772–81.

The present house dates from the mid-eighteenth century and its creation involved several renowned architects, artists and craftsmen. John Carr of York (born in Horbury) carried out the initial design of the house, which was started in 1759. He also designed the stables, farm and the new village houses. Harewood was his first great country house commission and it was here he assimilated first hand the style of Robert Adam. Adam, a Scottish architect, was responsible for much of the original interior decoration, with elaborate plasterwork, carpets and works of art, in which he was assisted by notable artists and craftsmen of the day. Thomas Chippendale of Otley, the famous furniture designer, made and supplied furnishings for the house, working closely with Edwin Lascelles and Adam.

In 1772 Lancelot 'Capability' Brown, the renowned landscape designer, was consulted. Over the next nine years he transformed the parkland in his inimitable English landscape style. Later, from 1800, Humphrey Repton carried out work, including the grand triumphal arch over the estate entrance.

Almost a century after its founding the house was altered by Louisa, Lady Harewood, and Sir Charles Barry, architect of the Houses of Parliament. The Italianate Terrace was added in the late 1840s and has recently been restored, creating a magnificent setting for the house.

4   Small is Beautiful

The Gothic
Temple,
Bramham Park
(mid-eighteenth
century). This is
a delightful tiny
building, one of
several within the
magnificent
eighteenth-
century
parkland.

Small buildings can be very appealing. From the diminutive Classical temples that grace the parklands of the great eighteenth-century houses to the tiny offices of the Leeds and Liverpool Canal Company, there exists a wide range of small buildings that are quite fascinating. Today there are very few opportunities to create 'tiny' architecture unless we include bus shelters!

Many of these minimal buildings are recognised by listing, including several that can broadly be described as lodges. The great country house parklands and the relatively smaller estates of the Victorians were normally

Above: Canal Company Office, Canal Wharf (1841). It is adjacent to Bridge 226, the first (or last) over the Leeds and Liverpool Canal. *Right:* Lodge to Bardon Hill, Weetwood Lane (1902). *Below:* Kippax Low Lodge, Barnsdale Road (early nineteenth century). This was the lodge to the former Kippax Park and is in a 'Gothick' style.

enclosed, with small entrance lodges as a first introduction to the 'big house' for visitors. So the architectural quality of the lodge was of great significance, serving to impress those who called.

Not only the great houses had entrance lodges. Public buildings such as universities, hospitals and cemeteries often had them for practical reasons. The advent of the car has seen the demise of many of these, while others have changed their original function.

In very few cases today are lodges still associated with their original 'parent' house, Ledston Hall Lodges being one example. Most have been engulfed by the spread of suburbia, the 'big house' demolished and its lands developed. The little lodges often survived only because of their location

Ledston Hall Lodges, Hall Lane. The entrance gates date from the late seventeenth century, the side lodges probably from the early eighteenth century.

Hook Moor Lodges, Main Street, Aberford. Attributed to John Carr of York, this is one of a pair formerly serving the now demolished Parlington Hall.

Cookridge Hospital Lodge, Hospital Lane (1868). It was designed by Richard Norman Shaw, the architect of New Scotland Yard, London.

Lodge to former Kirkstall Grange (Beckett's Park), 151 Otley Road. In a charming rustic style, it is built entirely in stone.

along roads fringing the original estate. Their ongoing survival now lies in the hands of a succession of interested and dedicated careful owners.

Remarkably, many of these small buildings display a considerable wealth of detail and decoration, with ornate chimney flues, intricately patterned slating, elaborate fretted bargeboards and clay tile ridge crestings. In contrast, on Otley Road can be seen a charming rustic lodge which is executed entirely in local sandstone, styled in the fashion of the *cottage ornée*.

Well-known architects did not overlook these small buildings. John Carr of York is said to have designed the Palladian Hook Moor Lodges on the Great North Road at Parlington. The eminent Richard Norman Shaw (architect of New Scotland Yard) created the tiny lodge at Cookridge Hospital in 1868.

5 Leeds Booms

The nineteenth century witnessed enormous changes, with industry, commerce and the social order accelerating at an incredible pace. New inventions and innovations changed the manner in which goods were produced, with a need for larger 'manufactories', buildings without precedent. The massive Park Mills in Leeds, the first of its kind in the world, was built as early as 1792 on what is now the Yorkshire Post Newspapers site on Wellington Street.

Proximity of local materials was an important factor prior to the arrival of the railways mid-century. The roads were in a terrible condition, particularly in winter. The second part of the century was to see a huge expansion and improvement of what we know today as 'infrastructure'.

Armley Industrial Museum, Canal Road (early eighteenth century). Formerly Armley Mills, it originally used water power for fulling and grinding corn. Benjamin Gott rebuilt it early in the nineteenth century, to produce woollen goods. Early fireproof construction with iron columns and beams with arched brick infill floors.

Former Round Foundry in Holbeck, Foundry Street, off Water Lane (1797). The tiny hamlet of Holbeck, across the Aire from the town, was to become the location for much of the early industry. Easy access to supplies of coal and the canal were crucial. The drawing gives an impression of how early engineering was carried out (leading to grievous pollution!). The foundry was founded in about 1797 for Fenton Murray and Wood. Only fragments remain today and the site is now being redeveloped as the mixed-use Holbeck Urban Village, preserving elements of historical significance.

The achievements of the engineers in the construction of roads, railways, bridges and canals were quite magnificent, undertaken with great speed. These were chaotic times; man was building for gain and competition was intense. Delay could prove costly.

Booming industries needed the support of business, banking and insurance. The growing population provided an ever-growing need for products, but there was also an increasing export trade. Many banks were opened to assist in trading and the development of the great diversity of industries.

Retail business expanded to serve the growing population, with markets moving from the streets into purpose-built structures. Shopping frontages were increased by the opening of covered arcades. Several were built in Leeds, and today form the core of the attractive city centre shopping area.

The architectural styles, designs and materials in use show great diversity. Though most industrial buildings were of relatively simple and traditional functional design, a few were enhanced by the use of Venetian, Egyptian or Italianate 'dressings'. Architects were perhaps more adventurous with domestic, commercial and religious structures. Banks, shops and churches were treated with a variety of historic styles of architecture, including Norman, Gothic and Classical. By contrast, the first Leeds Covered Market, 1857, was in cast iron and glass, its design clearly inspired by that of the Crystal Palace, in 1851 the most advanced building structure in the world of its time.

MADE IN LEEDS

The end of the eighteenth century witnessed the most dramatic and traumatic changes that Leeds had ever seen. The Industrial Revolution had arrived and with it a new type of building, the factory. The prosperity of the town was already well founded on the trading of wool cloth. The

The Hope Foundry, Mabgate (1831 onwards). The frontage is in an impressive Greek style.

vast profits of the merchants who finished and marketed the products of the locally based hand-loom weavers were invested in huge 'manufactories'. The whole process, from fleece to high-quality cloth, could now be realised under one roof, aided by the new steam engines powered by ample supplies of local coal. The cottage industry of spinning and weaving gradually diminished, many of the workers moving into the towns to become operatives in the factories. In 1792 Benjamin Gott built the world's first major integrated woollen mill at Bean Ing on the River Aire (now demolished). Over 1,000 workers are said to have been employed.

The Hunslet Engine Co., Jack Lane (1864). This is part of the frontage of the office block. Leeds had many engineering firms of international repute during the nineteenth century exporting all manner of products. This company was famous for its railway locomotives.

The wool cloth industry continued to flourish well into the nineteenth century and was joined by the first mechanised flax spinning mill in Holbeck. John Marshall built a series of factories, in which he was ably assisted by the inventive engineer, Matthew Murray. The engineering industry flourished, working closely with the textile factories, and Murray is also credited with the world's first successful commercial railway locomotive, used locally at Middleton Colliery. This and other inventions were built at the Round Foundry in Holbeck, established in 1797. Later in

the century, engineering was to become the town's most important industry, as most wool cloth production was to be largely lost to Bradford, and Belfast gained the ascendancy with the linen trade. The diversity of Leeds industry in this century was quite phenomenal. Fine buildings were erected for engineering, leather production, clothing firms and breweries in addition to the earlier wool and flax industries.

Early factories were sometimes badly built, using high unstable walls and timber floors. There were collapses due to vibration and the fire risk was high with loss of life. However, experience led to improvements involving the use of iron columns and beams with infill floors of brick arches, a form of 'fireproof' construction. This was used for John Marshall's flax mill in 1830 and at Armley Mills for Benjamin Gott. The former has an interesting advanced form of structure for its date. The early factories were built largely in the functional tradition and manner with no embellishment. However, the great wealth accumulated by some well-

New Crown Point Printing Works, Hunslet Road (c. 1894). Designed by Thomas Ambler, an early example of a purpose-built printing works. Cooke's specialised in colour printing from the 1880s.

known entrepreneurs was later to provide some magnificent monuments to industry and commerce, some unusual if not bizarre! And many of their architects looked abroad for inspiration.

John Marshall's Temple Mill is quite amazing. In its external appearance it looks back to the Pharaohs and Egypt. Architect Joseph Bonomi studied temples at Edfu and Karnak and adapted these for Holbeck. But it is in the

Temple Mill,
Marshall Street
(1838).

advanced building technology employed that the mill is forward looking. The huge single-storey production floor with its fireproof construction lit by sixty-five conical roof lights was a very rare, if not unique, creation for its time. The interior environment was controlled by an insulated flat roof with a soil and turf layer (upon which it is said that sheep once grazed). Other technical measures included internal climate control required for the flax processing. For the operatives, working conditions were far safer and healthier than those to be found in many other mills.

Tower Works, Globe Road, and its two Italianate towers. The earlier one (on right) is a chimney modelled on a Veronese structure. The larger one is a dust extraction shaft reminiscent of the Florence Cathedral campanile.

The former Smithfield Ironworks presents a handsome Classical frontage to North Street, Leeds. Only the entrance block to the former huge works has survived, its central clock tower the centre-piece of a multi-arched façade. Steam and road rollers, lawnmowers and rollers were made here. The impressive Classical frontage of Tower Works in Holbeck screens the site of Harding's factory, which produced steel products for the textile industry. Said to have been the largest factory of its type in the world in the 1860s, it is the site of two unusual architectural features. The earlier one is a chimney seemingly modelled on a campanile of the Palazzo del Commune in Verona, Italy. It may have been influenced by a pattern book for factory chimneys by Sir Robert Rawlinson. Later William Bakewell designed the larger feature, this time a dust extraction shaft whose design is based on Giotto's fourteenth-century campanile on the Florence *duomo*, again in Italy.

John Barran founded the world-famous Leeds tailoring industry with the mass production of ready-made clothing. Employing the new inventions of

Leeds was well known for its diversity of industries. Two examples. *Top:* Sugarwell Works, Meanwood Road (1866). Originally known as Cliff Tannery, it was one of many in Meanwood Valley producing leather. *Below:* Smithfield Ironworks, North Street (*c.* 1848–50). Steam and road rollers, lawn mowers and rollers were made here by Thomas Green & Sons, a leading engineering firm.

St Paul's House, 20–22 St Paul's Street (1878).

the Singer sewing machine and cloth cutting band-knife, he built a magnificent factory and warehouse. This is now known as St Paul's House. Architect Thomas Ambler looked to Spain for his inspiration and the building is Moorish in style with details similar to those on the great Islamic Alhambra Palace, Granada. Bright colours predominate, with buff terracotta, red brick and blue glazed tiles. The roof line is amazing with pierced profiled parapets and corner minarets. It was originally in brick and terracotta, but much has been replicated in glass fibre owing to frost damage. It is truly a very memorable building.

THE ENGINEERS

As industry in Holbeck and Hunslet grew rapidly in the early nineteenth century, there was a need for better access to and from the town centre across the River Aire. Between 1837 and 1873 three fine bridges were built that are still in use today at Neville Street, Bridge End and Crown Point. The first, Victoria Bridge, 1837–9, has a graceful flat arch in local sandstone and the others are in iron. However, probably the earliest iron

Leeds Bridge, Bridge End (1871–3). In cast iron, it replaced the medieval stone structure.

Two contrasting bridges by George Leather and Son. *Top:* Crown Point Bridge, Crown Point Road (1842). This is in Gothic style with open ironwork sides. *Right:* Victoria Bridge, Neville Street (1837–9). This is in local sandstone with central cartouche on the parapet celebrating 'VICTORIA'.

Seven Arches Aqueduct, Scotland Wood, Meanwood Park (*c.* 1840). By George Leather, it crossed Meanwood Beck, but was only in use for some ten years before it was replaced by a pipeline.

bridge in the area is at Newlay, Horsforth, over the Aire and built by John Pollard in 1819. Another interesting structure is the Seven Arches Aqueduct in the Meanwood Valley, *c*. 1840. This carried water from Eccup to Headingley, providing the town with its first good quality water supply.

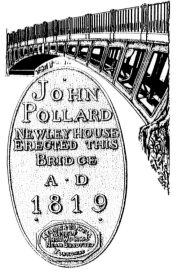

Iron Bridge, Horsforth, Newlay Lane (1819). By John Pollard, this is one of the oldest iron bridges in the country.

The opening of the canal network presented further challenges to the engineers, fine examples including locks, retaining walls and Bridge 226 in Leeds Canal Basin. The arrival of the railways in the second half of the century was to present even more rigorous demands on their ingenuity and skills. The Leeds and Thirsk Railway opened in 1849, traversing the valleys and high lands north of the town. There were many civil engineering problems involving bridges, cuttings, viaducts and the Bramhope Tunnel. Engineer Thomas Grainger was responsible for the design and construction of the Kirkstall and Arthington viaducts, magnificent structures and landscape features.

Canal Bridge 226, Canal Wharf (1841). On the west side of the Canal Basin, this is just one of some fine engineering works at the eastern end of the Leeds and Liverpool Canal.

BUSINESS MATTERS

Leeds and its hinterland developed into one of the world's greatest industrial centres during the nineteenth century, all manner of things being produced, from clothing to chemicals and leather to locomotives. Expanding business for both home consumption and export gave rise to a growing need for what is today known as the service industry, institutions such as banks, insurance companies and legal firms. This commercial sector signalled changes that were to continue into the present day, with Leeds now a major European centre for legal and financial services.

Industry employed huge numbers of workers. The population grew from 50,000 in 1801 to nearly 450,000 in 1911, an incredible ninefold increase. Working men and their families had to be fed and clothed, so there was a considerable increase in the provision of retail shopping and market facilities. The foundation was thus laid for today's nationally renowned city centre shopping, dining and entertainment attractions.

The first bank in Leeds had been opened in 1758, John Beckett later taking control. Early banks were locally based, serving the needs of the clothing industry. However, as the town grew in importance the Bank of England built a branch in South Parade, 1862–4. This was in a Greek Revival style with a distinctive key patterned frieze and open parapet with balusters and urns. It was a rather sober but robust building befitting its function of security. The last decade of the century witnessed the opening of

Below, left:
Sovereign House, 123 South Parade (1862–4).
This is the former Bank of England by P.C. Hardwick.
Below, right:
Former Midland Bank, 40 Boar Lane (1899). It was designed by W.W. Gwyther in a Classical style.

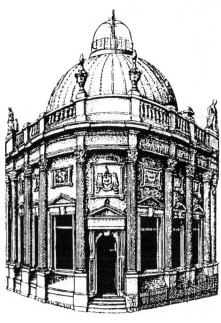

several more banks. The former Yorkshire Penny Savings Bank, 1894, was built in the Gothic Revival style, complete with gargoyles, but William Williams, Brown and Co. (the former Lloyds building) preferred a French style, with its steeply pitched château-like roof. The Classical style was not entirely ignored by the banks, with the former Midland Bank in City Square, 1899, gracing its curved corner with Corinthian columns and green copper dome.

Italy provided the precedents for the design of other commercial buildings. Starbucks now occupies the former insurance premises in Albion Street, which is in a Venetian palazzo style, 1852–5, with elaborate rustication to its ground floor. O'Neills pub was originally the Masonic Hall, whose upper windows and parapets are distinctly Venetian Gothic, 1866. Hepper House, 1863, is basically Gothic in style, but influences from other earlier architectural periods are featured.

The compact nature of city centre shopping is largely due to the creation of the network of arcades. With existing street frontages already fully taken up with shops, new provision was created by building covered arcades along the line of the medieval burgage plots which were the site of

Above, left: Former Insurance Co. Offices, 48 Albion Street (1852–5). Now a Starbucks Coffee Shop, it was designed by W.B. Gingell with Robert Mawer (sculptor).

Above, right: Former Lloyds Bank, 31–32 Park Row (1898). It was built for William Williams, Brown & Co., the architect being Alfred Waterhouse.

Former Masonic Hall, 24–26 Great George Street (1866).
Designed by Perkin & Sons, it is now a public house.

Hepper House, 17a East Parade (1863). It was designed by
George Corson in a Gothic style.

General Post Office, City Square (1896), on the left of the photograph. The architect was Sir Henry Tanner.

Two door portals in a Venetian style. *Far left:* Britannia Buildings, 4 Oxford Place (*c.* 1868). *Left:* Former Warehouse, 30 York Place (*c.* 1870).

traditional yards and courts. The earliest arcade was built by Charles Thornton in 1878 and takes his name for its title. It is tall and narrow, and rather austere in character in comparison with later arcades. Gothic arches line its three-storey sides, the roof carried by iron arches of horseshoe profile. A feature of all the arcades is that of the natural light from glazed roofs providing good conditions for shoppers, sheltered from the elements. Glazed atriums are still popular with today's architects!

Leeds Library, 16–20 Commercial Street (1808). Faced in stucco, this building in a Greek Regency style was designed by Thomas Johnson.

Some Victorian commercial buildings by Leeds Bridge. *Left:* Aire and Calder Navigation Warehouses along Dock Street (now housing). *Centre:* Riverside warehouses (now housing). *Right:* Leeds Bridge House (1880) has an early cast-iron frame. It was built as a temperance hotel and is now in shop and office use.

Further arcades followed, all rather more elaborate and colourful. The Grand Arcade, 1897, is rather plain internally, but street façades are rich and ornate, with terracotta and Burmantofts glazed ceramics. Its twin arches were originally entries into double arcades, the northern one now infilled. The design of the external façades, similar in both New Briggate and Vicar Lane, was influenced by the Art Nouveau movement, which advocated the use of the naturalistic flowing lines and curves found in plants and the like.

Thornton's Arcade, Briggate and Lands Lane (1878).

6   *Cuthbert Brodrick*

Of all the many fine civic buildings erected in the nineteenth century none symbolized emerging provincial civic pride better than did the magnificent Leeds Town Hall, surely the finest of its type in the country. Its creator was a young architect, Cuthbert Brodrick, from Hull. He won an open competition in 1852, which was judged by the eminent architect Sir Charles Barry, who had just designed the Houses of Parliament. Brodrick had designed few buildings outside Hull, but his success was the start of a fruitful architectural association with Leeds,

Leeds Town Hall.

Leeds Town Hall, Victoria Square, The Headrow
(1858).

including three 'landmark' structures of national importance. Other than
these he was responsible for few buildings outside Leeds, apart from the
massive Grand Hotel at Scarborough, 1862–7 and Wells House Hydro,
Ilkley, 1853–8. He was unsuccessful with architectural competition entries
for major buildings including the War Office, National Gallery and
Manchester Town Hall. He ceased practising in 1869, leaving to live in
France, and he died in Jersey in 1905.

Brodrick had toured Europe, admiring French Classical architecture, and
this was to influence his later designs. The construction of the Town Hall
commenced in 1853 using local millstone grit. The Corporation initially
decided to omit Brodrick's magnificent tower and dome. However,
three years later it was decided to proceed with this, so realising his
original concept in full. The building was conceived on a massive scale, its
colonnade of Corinthian columns and huge side pavilions raised well above
ground level on a strongly rusticated base. A wide flight of steps provides
an impressive and grandiose entrance to the monumental Baroque
composition. The principal feature of the interior is, of course, the
wonderful Victoria Hall. Its vaulted cylindrical ceiling and flanking
Corinthian columns are colourful and richly decorated, the main focus
being the great organ above the tiered seating and stage.

The construction of two further major buildings commenced in 1860, the Corn Exchange and the Mechanics Institute (now the Civic Theatre but soon to be a museum). Leeds had become an important railway centre and this enabled the town to retain and enhance its links with a large agricultural hinterland. Farmers and merchants had easy access to the greatly improved facilities provided by the new Corn Exchange, where trading in their produce could be carried out in ideal conditions. Brodrick had again won with his competition entry and he created the unique and majestic elliptical structure covered with a vast dome. The outer walls are punctuated by continuous bands of round-arched windows on two levels, capped with a heavy cornice and parapets. A distinctive feature of the masonry is the rustication with diamond-shaped modelling of the stone blocks, providing an interesting texture. The dome has two sections of roof glazing, with natural lighting being necessary for the trading in grains and cereals. The roof structure is of radiating iron arches which run in two directions at right angles, each intersection having cross bracing. The roof has a lightness and delicacy contrasting strongly with the heavy masonry enclosing walls.

The Corn Exchange, Call Lane (1862).

Above and below, left: Leeds Civic Theatre, Cookridge Street (1862), formerly the Mechanics' Institute.

Brodrick's Buildings, 49–51 Cookridge Street (1864).

A house in
Headingley,
7 Alma Road
(1859).

The third major building designed by Brodrick in Leeds is the Mechanics'
Institute. The movement for 'self-improvement' through education led to
the founding of several institutes in the towns of the area during the early
nineteenth century. Most working men did not receive formal education in
their early lives and the institutes offered a chance to 'catch up' and
improve themselves. They were, in a sense, the foundations of today's
further education colleges, and were funded by local benefactors and
philanthropists. French influences are very evident in Brodrick's design,
with the basement walls forming a high battered and rusticated plinth
expressing great strength and stability in the support of the massive stone
structure above. There are the familiar round arched windows, above
which is a tall modelled masonry wall with heavy cornice and parapet. At
the centre of the main façade a monumental deeply recessed archway gives
access to the Institute, above which a steeply pitched pavilion roof
accentuates the strongly symmetrical form of the building.

Some other important buildings designed by Cuthbert Brodrick have been
demolished, including the Oriental Baths (formerly opposite the Mechanics'

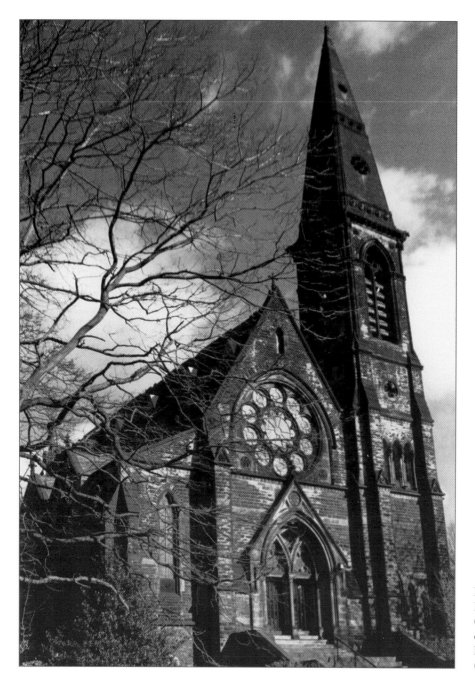

Former
Headingley Hill
Congregational
church,
Headingley Lane
(1864).

Institute) and a large warehouse in King Street, Leeds. However, 'lesser'
survivors include shops and offices (again opposite the Institute) and an
attractive villa in Headingley, 1859. The former Headingley Hill
Congregational church, 1866, was a solitary venture into the ecclesiastical
field, its main feature a large rose window in the west gable.

7   Civic Pride

Nineteenth-century Leeds was the ideal location for new industries and commerce, becoming a magnet for those men with initiative and talent. Many 'incomers' became more prosperous than the older classes, who had run the town for many years without significant change or improvement. Political change was necessary and this came in 1835 when the Liberals were elected after the passing of the Municipal Reform Act. They were to control the town (later the city) for sixty years. The period was one of massive development in all manner of public services, education and health as well as such basics as roads, bridges and sewers. There was an increasing pride in Leeds, with confidence in the future culminating with the visit of Queen Victoria to open the Town Hall in 1858. The great industrial towns of Leeds, Manchester, Liverpool and Birmingham were of great economic significance in the growing wealth of the country.

The growth of the population with the spread into the suburbs created problems for the various religious faiths. Nonconformism was popular early in the period following Wesley's preaching in the eighteenth century, but with the establishment of the Ripon diocese many new churches were built in outer suburbs. Catholicism attracted more worshippers with many immigrants from Ireland, St Anne's becoming one of the several new Roman Catholic cathedrals established in the great industrial cities. Jewish immigrants from Eastern Europe came to Leeds, founding several synagogues later in the century.

Social and health care early in the century was largely a task for the charitable trusts through churches or public benefactors. However, with public provision from around 1850, considerable strides were made, with a Workhouse, Industrial School and Fever Hospital being built in Burmantofts. These eventually formed part of St James's Hospital, at one time the largest in Europe. Leeds General Infirmary was built in the 1860s to a revolutionary new design and layout for hospitals. The two hospitals are today of international importance in many aspects of medicine.

The later Victorian period witnessed great advances in education at all levels. Perhaps most significant was the building of many 'Board' Schools for elementary pupils from 1870, with the provision of secondary education later. Such developments were publicly funded for the first time, as were the hospitals. The University of Leeds had its origins in the Yorkshire College founded later in the century. Prior to this adult education was provided by the Mechanics' Institute, of which there were several in the Leeds district.

CIVIC PRIDE

In 1835 Parliament reformed the ways in which local government, through the municipal corporations, was to administer the affairs of the many growing towns. From this time selected assemblies were created, so allowing greater participation by the middle classes. We thus have the beginnings of today's city and district councils, with the town halls offering an important local facility and amenity.

The earliest existing town hall in the district is in Wetherby, dating from 1845. It is in a simple Classical style with a clock set within the three-bay pediment above the entrance. Leeds Town Hall was opened in 1858, designed by the eminent architect Cuthbert Brodrick. Yeadon Town Hall, 1879–80, is in a severe French Gothic style with steeply pitched roofs. Morley Town Hall, 1892–5, was seemingly influenced by the design of Leeds, and there are similar buildings in Bolton and Portsmouth.

Queen Victoria opens the Town Hall in 1858.

WETHERBY

LEEDS

The four town halls of Leeds.
Clockwise from top left:
Wetherby: Market Place (1845);
Leeds: The Headrow (1858);
Yeadon: High Street, architect
   William Hill (1880);
Morley: Queen Street, architect
   G.A. Fox (1895).

YEADON

MORLEY

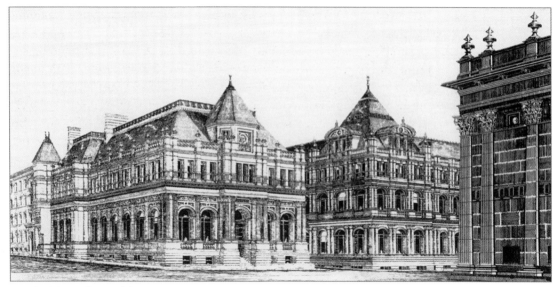

Two buildings designed by George Corson. *Left:* Civic Court, Calverley Street (1880), originally the offices of the Leeds School Board. *Centre:* Leeds Central Library, Calverley Street (1876), formerly the Municipal Buildings, and prior to this called the Public Offices. *Right:* The north-eastern corner of the Town Hall.

The roof line of the Civic Court (far left), and of the Central Library.

Architectural details at the Leeds Central Library. Staircase decoration (left), and ironwork railings and Leeds owls.

Initially, Leeds Town Hall housed a wide variety of functions, including police station, law courts, offices for town clerk and borough surveyor and, of course, the magnificent public hall. As municipal businesses increased, new buildings were needed and new 'Public Offices' (later Municipal Buildings and now the Central Library) were built in 1876. Adjacent to the Town Hall, this building is in a French–Italian style, its three-storey mass with dramatic roofline harmonising with its famous neighbour. The interior has some magnificent features including an open stairwell treated with rich colourful materials and sculpture. Adjoining this building are the former School Board Offices, 1880, which are in a similar style to the Central Library. The main entrance is very impressive, up the steps between two pairs of Corinthian columns and under the high arched recessed porch, flanked by sculptures of a schoolboy and schoolgirl within small niches.

WORSHIP

In the first half of the nineteenth century there was intense rivalry between the various religious denominations in Leeds and its outer townships. Nonconformist chapels considerably outnumbered the Established churches, with Methodism having flourished for almost a century. One

Wetherby Wesleyan Methodist Chapel, Bank Street (1829).

factor in this had been the division and fragmentation of the faith into a number of different sects such as the Wesleyans, Primitives and New Connexion, with each building their own chapels. Unitarians, Baptists and the Society of Friends also built chapels locally. These groups usually favoured building in a simple neat Classical style following the precedents from the Georgian period, using little ornamentation or decoration. The very plain Wesleyan chapel in Wetherby, 1829, is an early example. Later, wealthier congregations endowed new buildings in the Gothic Revival style such as Mill Hill Chapel, City Square, 1848. In this they followed the Church of England, which was building using various interpretations of the Gothic.

The Anglicans were concerned about their lack of appeal to the fast growing population, but one man was to revive their spiritual 'fortunes'. The Revd Dr Hook was responsible for the present Leeds Parish Church, 1839–41, with architect R.D. Chantrell, who designed in a Gothic Revival manner influenced by the Decorated period. Dr Hook's personal appeal attracted very large congregations during a twenty-two-year incumbency, but his major contribution to the new Ripon diocese was to oversee the founding of several new Anglican churches to serve the growing suburban population.

Parish Church of St Peter, Kirkgate (1841).

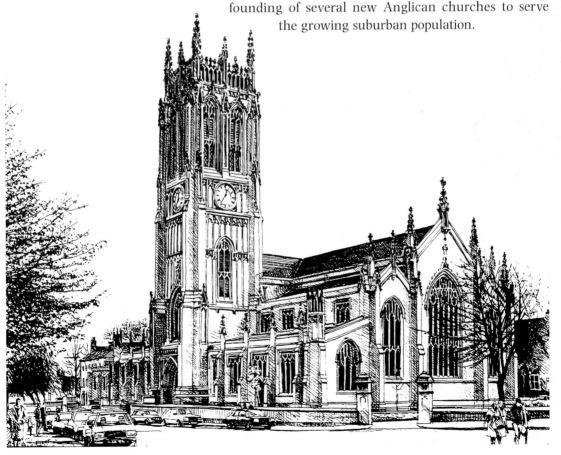

The growing influx of the Irish, attracted by booming industry, led to the building of the huge Mount St Mary's Roman Catholic church on Richmond Hill, 1857. Cathedral-like in scale, it seated 2,000 and is a notable landmark in east Leeds. It was designed by John Hansom, who was also responsible for the horse-drawn cab. Hansom also prepared drawings for the Roman Catholic church of St Edward in Clifford, 1845–8, an essay in the Norman Romanesque Revival. Its distinctive high tower is unusual in that it has an open porch below, at ground level.

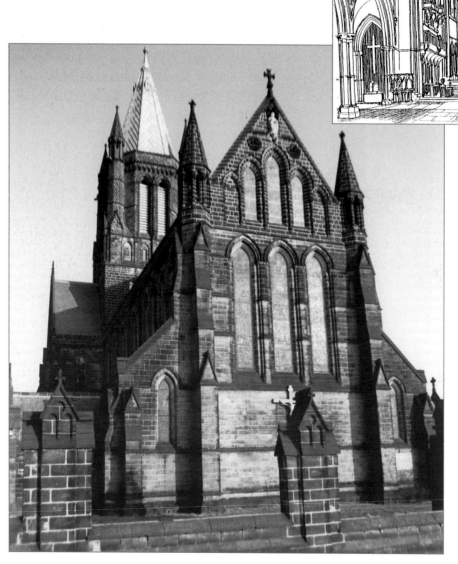

The church of St Bartholomew, Strawberry Lane (1872). A prominent landmark in west Leeds, it was designed by Walker and Athron.

Mount St Mary's, Church Road (1857).

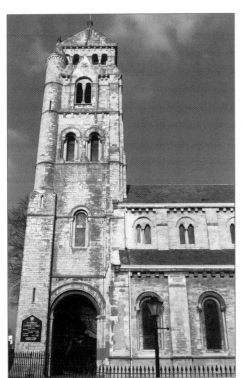
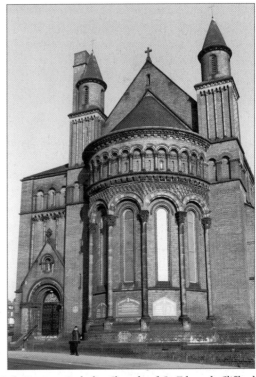

Two churches in the Romanesque (round-arched) style. *Left:* Roman Catholic Church of St Edward, Clifford (1848). *Right:* Church of St Aidan, Roundhay Road (1894), by R.J. Johnson and A. Crawford-Hick. Internally, the eastern apse has fine mosaics by Sir Frank Brangwyn.

Social Reforms

Almshouses for the old and needy were to be found in many towns and villages, most founded well before the nineteenth century. They were built and endowed by churches, charities, the levy of 'poor rates' or local benefactors such as John Harrison, the Leeds merchant. In 1845 one of distinctive and unique design was endowed by the Gascoigne family of Parlington Park, Aberford. Grandiose and church-like, it has ten gables and turrets, with a high central tower, all in a Gothic style. Curiously, it housed only eight elderly people! Other notable groups include St John's Almshouses, Roundhay, which includes a school at its centre, 1830, and at All Saints Church, Ledsham.

The Poor Law Act of 1834 reinstituted workhouses where the 'able-bodied poor' could be 'usefully' occupied. Those who found themselves destitute (mainly because of unemployment) dreaded having to enter workhouses that were austere, almost prison-like, and where a harsh regime was employed so as to deter the feckless and the idle. The Leeds Union Workhouse, 1861, is an impressive building in Elizabethan Gothic style that accommodated 800 paupers. In 1925 it became part of St James's Hospital and today houses the Thackray Medical Museum.

The Gascoigne Almshouses, Aberford, Main Street (1845), designed by the architect G.F. Jones for Mary and Elizabeth Gascoigne.

St John's School
and Almshouses,
Wetherby Road,
Roundhay
(*c.* 1830), designed
by Thomas Taylor
for Stephen
Nicholson of the
Mansion,
Roundhay.

Thackray Medical
Museum,
St James's Hospital,
Beckett Street
(1858). The former
Leeds Union
Workhouse was
designed by Perkin
and Backhouse.

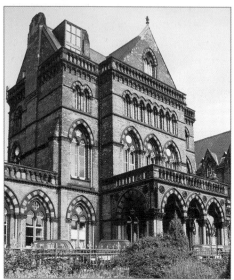

Leeds General Infirmary, Great George Street, designed by Sir G. Gilbert Scott in 1868, and later extended by George Corson in 1892, and by Kitson and Parish in 1917. *Below*: Cookridge Hospital, Hospital Lane (1868).

The fast growing population required the building of more hospitals later in the century. Two of these were built at about the same time by well-known architects, and present great contrasts in their architectural treatment. G.G. Scott's Leeds General Infirmary, 1862–8, is in a severe pointed Gothic Revival style, while Richard Norman Shaw's Cookridge Convalescent Hospital, 1868, is Swiss-chalet like, with large gabled dormers and upper walls finished with red tile hanging. Shaw's design could well have been built a century later, such is its modern appearance.

LEARNING IN LEEDS

Meanwood Church of England Primary School, Green Road (1840).

The education of working-class children during the early nineteenth century was initially provided by charitable institutions, religious denominations or individual benefactors such as Christopher Beckett of Meanwood Park. He built and maintained the local village school in 1840, retaining ownership. He also paid the staff until his death in 1847, after which the school was conveyed to church ownership. In local stone, it has pointed arch windows, steeply pitched roofs and a bell turret, all strongly Gothic. The tiny charming former North Leeds School in Gledhow, Leeds, 1872, is in a similar style. Again, it was administered by the local church 'for the education of the poor of the area'. Similar early church schools can

North Leeds School
at Gledhow,
Gledhow Lane
(1873).

be seen in Oulton, 1877, and at St John's, Roundhay. The government did
grant aid to the voluntary schools so as to encourage development, but
until 1870 there was no comprehensive provision for education.

The 1870 Elementary Education Act, while encouraging the voluntary
schools to expand, called for state schools to be built where needed. In
Leeds, the need was great with such a fast growing population and high
birth rates. The Leeds School Board was formed in 1870 (hence the 'Board
Schools' – later to become the 'Council Schools'). The Board was to achieve
great success in its provision of new schools. Thirty-one large schools were
built up to 1878, while by 1902 (when Leeds Corporation took over its
role) over 160 had been handed over to the newly created Education
Committee.

The Board's architect, Richard Adams, designed many of the earlier schools. These were in a variety of architectural styles, though the need for economy was to lead to the adoption of standard plans and details. The Chapel Allerton Board School, 1878, has much in common with the earlier voluntary schools, but a notable change is in the window design with

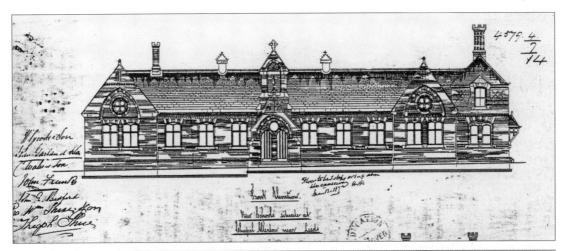

Above: Chapel Allerton Primary School, Harrogate Road (1878). This is one of the architect's drawings for the front elevation by Richard Adams.

Two former Board Schools in west Leeds. *Centre:* Adams Court (Council Offices), Kildare Terrace (1884). The former school was designed by Richard Adams. *Bottom:* Tower Court, Armley Road. The former school was designed by Adams and Kelly. The building is now in commercial use.

larger areas of glazing. The importance of fresh air and natural lighting is recognised with the adoption of high ceilings with tall wide windows. In New Wortley, a much larger school, 1884, is two storeyed with simplified window details and prominent chimney stacks. The design of this basic building was repeated elsewhere in the town. In contrast, the Armley Road Board School, 1878, is quite impressive, with a much more elaborate treatment. In an Italianate style, it is symmetrical with a high central clock tower surmounted by an open bell turret.

Two former secondary schools in Leeds. *Above:* Thoresby Building (Council Offices), Great George Street (1900). Formerly the Pupil Teachers College, Thoresby High School and City of Leeds Schools, this was designed by W.S. Braithwaite. *Left:* Council Offices, Woodhouse Lane (1889). Built for higher-grade pupils by Birchall and Kelly, this became the Leeds Central High School, and then the City of Leeds School.

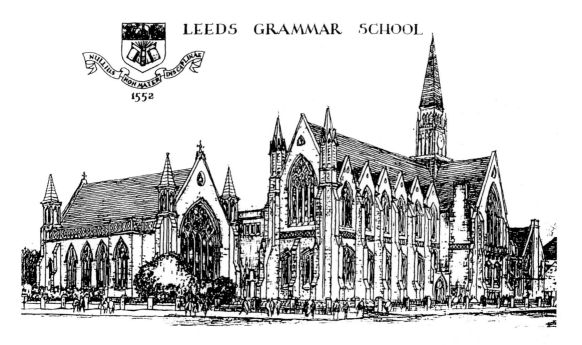

LEEDS GRAMMAR SCHOOL

1552

Former Leeds Grammar School, Moorland Road (1859), designed by E.M. Barry. The building is now in use by the University of Leeds.

In 1889 publicly funded secondary education was introduced with the opening of the impressive Central Higher Grade School in Leeds. A massive five-storey brick building with a roof top playground, it was in a 'stripped' Classical style with huge sliding sash windows. Apparently, some 2,500 children were in attendance! At the turn of the century, the new Pupil Teachers College was built adjacent to the Central using a similar Classical treatment but having a more elaborate roof line. Two pediments infilled with carved decoration and two copper covered ogee roofs cap the twin staircase towers, presenting a lively and interesting skyline. In recent years these two schools housed the postwar city of Leeds School.

For the middle classes, fee-paying education was available at the Leeds Grammar School, which was established early in the seventeenth century, near to St John's Church (New Briggate). A major move to a more pleasant location near Woodhouse Moor was made in 1859. E.M. Barry designed the new school in a lively Gothic Revival manner, a style adopted by many contemporary public schools. It was considered that a Christian education was best pursued in an environment echoing life in the Middle Ages.

The Mechanics' Institutes had a major role in adult and technical education, ranging in size from the tiny Meanwood Institute, 1870, to Cuthbert Brodrick's magnificent academy in Cookridge Street. A wide range of practical and vocational subjects were taught and many had libraries. Horsforth, 1881, and Otley, 1870, have handsome civic-scale buildings that still function today as public meeting places, offering facilities for all manner of education and social activities.

Meanwood Institute, Green Road (*c.* 1840).

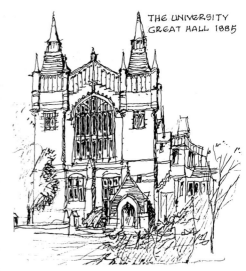

THE UNIVERSITY
GREAT HALL 1885

Above and opposite: The Great Hall, University of
Leeds, University Road (1877–1912). One of
the first buildings for the Yorkshire College, it
was designed by Alfred Waterhouse.

Horsforth Mechanics' Institution, Town Street
(1881). The building is now in use as a library
and community centre.

The Yorkshire College was formed late in the nineteenth century, becoming the University of Leeds in 1904. The College appointed Alfred Waterhouse to design the original range of buildings in a mild Gothic style, using hard red brick with dressings of local stone. The Great Hall, 1891–4, has a huge traceried window between the towers and turrets capped with steep slated pyramidal roofs. The south gable has a strictly symmetrical façade except for the arched entrance porch. Curiously, this is offset to the right! Overall, this range of 'redbrick' displays great character and dignity in a familiar collegiate style.

8   Clockwise

Clocks are prominent and fascinating features of the Leeds townscape. It is interesting that a Darlington man, William Potts, moved to Pudsey in 1832, founding a clockmaker's business which was to flourish with mutual benefits for the firm and the booming town during the Victorian era. There was a huge demand for clocks on prestige buildings and William Potts and Sons were to become the leading British clockmakers. Most of the clocks illustrated were made by the firm which is still based in Leeds after nearly 170 years.

One of the most elaborate clocks produced was for John Dyson, the Briggate jewellers, watch and clockmaker. Above the main clock 'Time Balls'

The Jubilee Clock, Otley Market Place (1887).

Time Ball Building, Lower Briggate. The building is possibly mid-eighteenth century in origin but its façade was enhanced a century or so later. A unique and charming 'temple to the measurement of time', it is now in use as a restaurant.

Thornton's Arcade, Briggate and Lands Lane (1878). The first of the Leeds arcades has this fine mechanical tableau, which has delighted many generations of Leeds children.

Grand Arcade, New Briggate and Vicar Lane (1897). This animated clock within the arcade was designed by Smith and Tweedale.

Two 'civic' clocks from different eras. *Left:* General Post Office, City Square (1896). Designed by Henry Tanner, the building contrasts strongly with its more recent neighbours. *Right:* Leeds Civic Hall, Calverley Street (1933). This is one of two bracket clocks flanking the front elevation of the Civic Hall.

were dropped precisely at noon daily to the acclamation of shoppers and passengers on passing tramcars. The creation of the famous shopping arcades provided further opportunities for the Potts clock designers. In 1878, in Thornton's Arcade a scene from Sir Walter Scott's *Ivanhoe* was created with figures by sculptor J.W. Appleyard. Later a similar feature was built at the east end of the Grand Arcade including a revolving platform with figures of a guardsman and a Highland soldier emerging from a rear compartment.

Leeds Town Hall and the General Post Office have magnificent clocks set high in the city centre. Other significant landmark clocks flank major highways such as Hunslet Road where the former Alf Cooke's printing

Two hospital clocks on 'Landmark' water towers. *Left:* Seacroft, York Road (1902–4). This was designed by E.T. Hall in a simple manner pointing the way towards an emerging new architecture for the twentieth century. *Right:* Former St George's, Wood Lane, Rothwell (late nineteenth century). This elaborate tower contrasts with that at Seacroft.

works dominates at a major junction. Another setting for public clocks arose through the building of hospitals late in the nineteenth century. Water towers were required providing an opportunity for prominent clock locations. At Seacroft Hospital a beautifully proportioned brick tower with Arts and Crafts influences is an attractive Leeds landmark. At Rothwell the former St George's Hospital tower has a rather Germanic feel with half-timbered capping above the brick arcaded shaft.

There are charming freestanding clock towers in Roundhay and Otley. The former originally stood within the City Markets in Vicar Lane but is now at Oakwood, its highly decorative and richly detailed form gracing the

entry to the open spaces of Roundhay
Park. In contrast Otley's Jubilee Clock
stands within the tight urban space of the
Market Place. The clock tower of local
sandstone is a well loved landmark in this
fine historic town.

Oakwood Clock Tower,
Roundhay Road. Originally
standing in Leeds Market, it
was made in 1904 by
William Potts & Sons to the
design of Leeming and
Leeming. It was moved here
in 1912.

9 Home & Hospitality

The great majority of working-class people in the nineteenth century endured dreadful social evils, living in squalid conditions in overcrowded towns. Later in the century bye-laws eased the problems, but still allowed the building of back-to-back houses in blocks of eight, four behind four. Behind each block was an open yard with privies. It is interesting that some of these houses are still occupied today, albeit with improved sanitation. After several outbreaks of cholera mid-century, a comprehensive network of sewers was installed and public health improved.

Wealthier people tended to move into areas further from the town centres, where they could live in individual dwellings or larger terraces, which continued the pattern established in the eighteenth century. The former were highly individualistic in a variety of styles, with 'pointed Gothic' very popular, in Venetian or Greek guise. Most had large gardens.

The railways allowed more people to travel around the country and several hotels were built close to the stations in Leeds, providing overnight and business accommodation. These gradually replaced the coaching inns of the eighteenth century, as such journeys were replaced by a more comfortable and speedy mode of travel. Pubs were to undergo radical changes during this time with larger premises being built, offering a variety of décor, 'atmosphere' and, of course, imbibers! In architectural terms the most interesting perhaps are those built at the end of the nineteenth century, catering for city-dwellers and having a wealth of expensive terracotta, tiles, etched glass, leather and hardwoods. Conversely, in historical terms there are many surviving examples of the traditional English pub in local towns and villages such as Otley and Wetherby, as well as the former coaching inns along the Great North Road.

Another form of leisure and entertainment, the theatre, was popular late in the Victorian era. In Leeds only two remain in use today, the City Varieties and the Grand Theatre. The former is the famous music hall, which retains the original auditorium seen by millions in the TV series *The Good Old Days*. A contemporary critic described the Grand Theatre as 'not one of the most handsome buildings in Leeds, externally'. However, he goes on to say that 'internally it is one of the finest and handsomest out of London but will well repay the sight-seer who visits it'. Opening in 1878, it originally accommodated almost 3,000 persons and is one of Britain's finest Victorian theatres.

HOMES

The Industrial Revolution brought about unprecedented social changes, including the emergence of a much larger middle-class population. Although the influence of the established aristocracy was still important,

Two mansions designed by Sir Robert Smirke. *Below:* Oulton Hall Hotel, Oulton Park (*c.* 1822). *Bottom:* Armley House, Armley Ridge Road (*c.* 1829). (The wings are now demolished.)

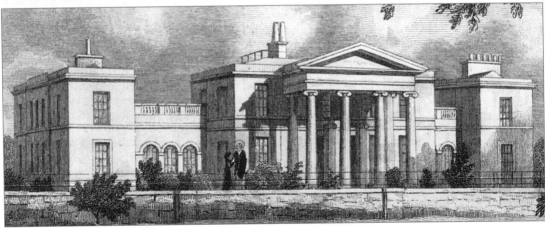

Two mansions designed by John Clark. *Right:* Mansion Hotel, Roundhay, Mansion Lane (*c.* 1826). *Below:* Fairbairn House, 71–75 Clarendon Road (1841).

Blenheim Terrace, 2–26 Woodhouse Lane (*c.* 1830–9).

Two Headingley houses in contrasting styles. *Above:* North Hill House, North Grange Mount (1846). *Left:* Hilton Court, 2 North Hill Road (*c.* 1840).

Spenfield, Otley
Road (1876),
designed by
George Corson.

there were to be fewer large country estates with their grandiose houses. Impressive Classical-style mansions were built at Roundhay, 1826, and Oulton, 1822, prior to the accession of Queen Victoria, but after this houses for more wealthy patrons were modest in scale. Many middle-class families moved to escape from the increasingly squalid conditions that existed in town centres. Initially, speculative builders catered for their needs, offering dignified houses for rental. Following the eighteenth-century Georgian-style Parks Estates, some fifty years later fine Classical terraces were built in the Woodhouse area of Leeds, notably Blenheim Terrace, 1830 onwards.

Some of the more wealthy of the business and professional classes aspired to detached villas with gardens in even more pleasant areas such as Headingley, Potternewton and Roundhay. Headingley Hill was popular in mid-century. North Hill House, 1846, is in the Gothic style with Tudor Jacobean influences in its battlements and pinnacles. Nearby, Hilton Court, 1840, is in Greek Classical style. This era was known for the 'Battle of the Styles' (architecturally of course). It was the Classical versus the Gothic. The former was prevalent when the century opened, but by mid- to late nineteenth century the 'pointed Gothic' was preferred by many clients and their architects for new dwellings.

Opposite: Spenfield, entrance detail.

Bardon Hill, Weetwood Lane (1875).

Far Headingley and Weetwood have several minor mansions in Gothic style. Spenfield, 1876, is rather plain and severe externally, but has magnificent decorative interiors. Bardon Hill, 1873, by contrast, has a highly exuberant exterior. Steeply pitched pointed gables, fretted bargeboards and a central tower with open pyramidical roof complete a picture of High Victorian splendour. Such architectural virtuosity was not for all, however, and should be seen against a background where the majority of the 'lower orders' of society lived in dire poverty in the town's squalid and overcrowded slums.

'Bye-law' housing, Inner Leeds. For the 'lower orders' of society many thousands of such back-to-backs were built in the late nineteenth and early twentieth centuries.

HOSPITALITY

Opposite:
Bardon Hill.

Hotels and Entertainment

The public house provides a popular place of refreshment, recreation and relaxation for millions every day. They vary widely in their planning, design and style, depending on location and the needs of their clientele. First, the coaching inns in the first half of the century. The Great North Road linked London and Edinburgh long before the A1–M1 was created. The road ran along the eastern edge of the present Leeds district passing through Aberford and Wetherby, and prior to the arrival of the railway era it was very busy, with horse-drawn stage coaches. In the 1820s the journey from York to London took about twenty hours, so there was a need for overnight stops en route, which were provided by the many coaching inns. Several still exist, albeit performing a different role. The Swan Inn at Aberford has the former stables through its central archway. In Wetherby, the Angel (with stabling for 100 horses) and the Swan and Talbot were busy inns, contributing to the town's prosperity. In Leeds, several coaching inns existed in Briggate, but these have been either demolished or radically altered.

Below: Swan Hotel, Main Street, Aberford (late eighteenth century). This former coaching inn has original stables through the archway.

In Briggate, the historic street markets were served by many taverns down the yards and courts. The Ship, Pack Horse and Whitelocks (Turks Head Tavern) are part of Leeds folklore. The latter is housed in a row of traditional cottages, much altered. The low-ceilinged interior is magnificent, with colourful ceramic tiling, marble, copper, brass and etched mirrors. Behind Leeds Town Hall, the 'Vic', properly the Victoria Hotel, 1865, served those attending the Assize Courts and retains many interior features. In the suburbs, the fine Cardigan Arms, 1893, in Kirkstall Road has its original brewhouse to the rear, with a dignified stone frontage. In Otley, the White Swan, 1899, has an interesting wide frontage with a large side archway leading to stables.

The turn of the century, into the Edwardian era, witnessed a new approach to pub design with the use of locally produced Burmantofts terracotta, faience and glazed ceramics. Apart from their attractive

Above: Whitelocks (Turks Head Tavern), Turks Head Yard (1886), a conversion of a row of early eighteenth-century cottages. The photograph shows its mirrored glass entrance door.

Cardigan Arms, 364 Kirkstall Road (1893).

White Swan,
Otley, Boroughgate
(1901).

Two south Leeds pubs faced with
terracotta and ceramics. *Right:* New
Inn, Dewsbury Road (*c.* 1900).

Left: Garden Gate, Whitfield Way (1902).

appearance, these materials were durable and easily cleaned, important in the heavily polluted streets. The New Inn, Dewsbury Road (1900), is faced with such materials and has wide arched windows with etched glass. But in Hunslet an even better example of a contemporary pub can be visited. The Garden Gate, 1902, is said to have been a small 'gin palace'. Its front elevations are similar to those of the New Inn but its details are more elaborate. Bronze and brown ceramics and faience are used externally but original interior features have also been retained and are of high quality. Behind the curved bar counter faced with green and yellow tiles is an elegant classical back bar fitting in carved timber. In all, it is a wonderful example of an early Edwardian city public house. The Jubilee Hotel, 1904, in The Headrow (now the Quo Vadis) is faced with red terracotta, as is the Metropole Hotel, 1899, in King Street. The latter is something of a *tour de force* with its highly modelled and richly decorated façade. Both these buildings have very fine Art Nouveau features on their façades.

The richly decorated interior of the Garden Gate.

Former Jubilee Hotel (now Quo Vadis), 167 The Headrow (1904). This was described as a 'gin palace' for the better-off imbiber.

Below: City Varieties Music Hall, Swan Street (1865). This was possibly designed by George Smith, who built Thornton's Arcade in 1878, his client being Charles Thornton of the Old Talbot Inn on Briggate.

The Grand Theatre, the auditorium.

Grand Theatre, 32–4 New Briggate (1878), designed by George Corson.

Two Leeds Victorian theatres are worthy of note, the City Varieties Music Hall, 1865, and the Grand Theatre, New Briggate, 1878. The former is modest and compact but retains its mid-Victorian character as personified by *The Good Old Days* of BBC TV fame. The Grand (as its name suggests) had seating for 2,600 in an exuberant and colourful interior, with its three horseshoe-shaped balconies under a magnificent ornate ceiling. Conversely, the exterior is not particularly inviting, being in a rather sober Romanesque style with a hint of the Scottish Baronial (the architect George Corson was a Scot).

10 In Memory

Barran drinking fountain, Roundhay Park (1882). It was presented to the Borough of Leeds by John Barran MP, who was instrumental in purchasing the park for the townspeople.

Our forebears erected many monuments and memorials for all manner of reasons, in mourning or celebration. Today many of these are forgotten, with time, weather, pollution and birds as relentless enemies (not to forget human graffiti 'artists'). However, the Leeds Lists include a variety of these, affording them a degree of protection for the future.

War memorials are likely to be the monuments we recall first, as these are usually located in busy public places. The Leeds Cenotaph in Victoria Square is probably the grandest example, aspiring to that in Whitehall by Sir Edwin Lutyens and the focus of our National Day of Remembrance. In Pudsey the 'British Tommy' stands high on a solid pillar of stone, fitting

Lest we forget – three Leeds war memorials. *Left:* Wetherby Bridge, High Street (*c.* 1920). E.F. Roslyn was the sculptor for this memorial, which is set on the parapet of the bridge, an ancient monument with thirteenth-century origins. *Centre:* Pudsey, Chapeltown (*c.* 1921), designed by Brierley and Rutherford (York) with sculptor Henry Poole of London. *Right:* The Cenotaph, The Headrow (1922). Originally in City Square and designed by J.E. Proctor, it was relocated here in 1937. The sculptor was Henry C. Fahr.

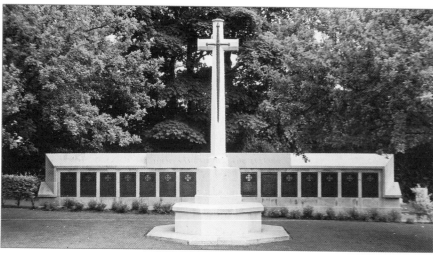

Lawnswood Cemetery, Otley Road. Laid out in about 1920, this resembles a miniature corner of the First World War 'Flanders fields'.

Bramhope Tunnel
Disaster Memorial,
All Saints
churchyard,
Kirkgate, Otley.
This scale model of
the tunnel portals
was erected to the
memory of 'the
unfortunate men'
killed during the
tunnel's
construction,
1845–9.

perfectly into the strong character of this fine Yorkshire town. By contrast, the graceful form of a winged angel set on Wetherby Bridge welcomes visitors to another attractive market town. Finally, for quiet contemplation why not visit Lawnswood Cemetery, where you will find a tiny piece of Flanders, limestone and bronze set in a trim greensward.

Some memorials are of unusual design. In Otley the replica of the Bramhope Tunnel portals carries an inscription dedicated to the 'unfortunate men' who died during its construction in the mid-nineteenth century. And in Beckett Street Cemetery, Thomas Kidney, 'the oldest steeplejack in England', lies under another replica, an industrial chimney in soot-blackened sandstone. But the most puzzling and poignant is the Lawnswood memorial to Edith Preston: she waits by the open door in a life-size open porch of limestone.

Above and left: The Kidney Memorial, Beckett Street Cemetery. Erected in about 1895, this was an appropriate memorial to Mr Kidney, who had climbed many similar (but full-size) structures during his working life.

Right: Edith Preston Memorial, Lawnswood Cemetery, Otley Road (1911), a memorial to the wife of Walter Preston. She stands in the porch in front of an open door. For whom is she waiting?

So far sadness and reflection have shaped the monuments featured, but now for some of a happier nature. Elementary education was introduced in Leeds in 1870 with the School Board offices built 1879–81. Flanking the main entrance steps are a pair of niches that house the carved stone figures of a schoolboy and schoolgirl of the time, the former dutifully carrying his books and slate – a fascinating insight into early school days.

Some monuments have a practical function, such as John Barran's drinking fountain in Roundhay Park. But perhaps the most impressive of Leeds statues is that of Queen Victoria. During her reign the city became

Civic Court
(former School
Board offices),
Calverley Street
(1881). This
sculpture of a
schoolboy flanks
the front
entrance.

Statue of Queen Victoria, Woodhouse Moor, Woodhouse Lane (1903). By George Frampton RA, this fine work was situated outside the Town Hall until 1937.

one of Britain's greatest centres of industry, business and commerce. Formerly standing outside the Town Hall (which she opened in 1858), her statue was moved to Woodhouse Moor. This fine work is surely deserving of full renovation and a more impressive location where it can be enjoyed by more people.

11   A Break with the Past

The roots of 'modern' architecture as we know it today can be traced back to the late nineteenth century. Towards the end of this period buildings that predicted a different future for architecture began to appear on the scene. These exemplars demonstrated that buildings that functioned well could also be beautiful. Simplicity was the keynote; there was no need for the decoration and ornament favoured by many architects of the day. The engineers had given the lead with structures that were honest and direct, expressing their function without resort to Classical columns or Gothic arches.

Ideas on architecture and building were being disseminated more readily with improved communications worldwide. Foreign influences from Europe and the United States began to play a part. The work of Frank Lloyd Wright in Chicago, Walter Gropius in Germany and Eliel Saarinen in Finland was watched with interest. These architects used a new generation of building materials such as steel, glass and concrete.

Two design movements were important during this period. The first was Arts and Crafts, which owed its existence to William Morris, artist and philosopher. An emphasis on the use of craftsmanship in the development of local vernacular building influenced the design of much housing of the day in garden cities and suburbs. The second movement was that of Art Nouveau. Its origins were in Western Europe but it was interpreted in very different styles by exponents Antonio Gaudi in Barcelona and Charles Rennie Mackintosh in Glasgow. The Art School designed by the latter is regarded as the most important building of the time, completed in 1896. Art Nouveau was short-lived, however, finding favour in Belgium, France and Austria, but with little impact in Britain.

Two houses by Bedford and Kitson Architects. *Below:* Lincombe, North Hill Road (1898), built for the Currer Briggs family. *Bottom:* Red Hill, 33 Shire Oak Road.

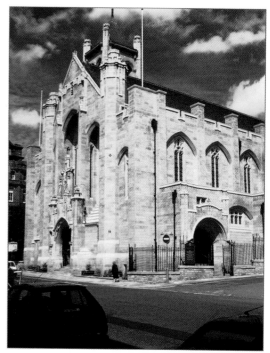

Top left: The Former Hostel of the Resurrection, Springfield Mount (1910), designed by Temple Moore and modelled on an Oxbridge college. It is now part of the University of Leeds. *Top right:* St Anne's Roman Catholic cathedral, Cookridge Street (1904), designed by J.E. Eastwood and S.K. Greenslade. *Left:* St Matthew's Church, Wood Lane, Chapel Allerton (1898), an Anglican church designed by G.F. Bodley.

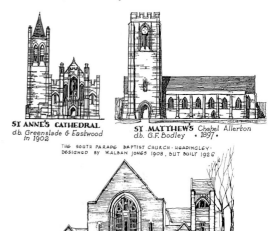

Churches in the Arts and Crafts tradition.

Historic styles continued into this period alongside the newly introduced movements. Most popular was a form of 'stripped-down' Classical, a simplified Georgian or Queen Anne Revival. This was considered a 'safe' way of treating public architecture that continued well into the twentieth century. But such buildings were constructed in quite a different manner from their historic precedents.

A DIFFERENT APPROACH?

The turn of the nineteenth century witnessed some remarkable and innovative changes in the design of buildings. High Victorianism continued beyond 1901, with many architects still creating buildings in one of the established historical Revival styles (amusingly, 'Classic for banks – Gothic for churches'). However, after the nineteenth century some architects (and engineers) produced architecture with quite a different approach, rejecting historic ornament and decoration. Further, political, philosophical and aesthetic movements began to influence design, as did the beginning of

Student residencies, Beckett Park (1911), designed by G.W. Atkinson for the City of Leeds Training College, the campus is now part of the Leeds Metropolitan University.

Centenary House, North Street (1904). The former Leeds Public Dispensary was designed by Bedford and Kitson.

'functionalism'. Eventually simplicity was to be the outcome, with individualism and romanticism gradually becoming less relevant. The twentieth-century 'Modern Movement' in architecture had its roots in the nineteenth century, perhaps inspired by the 1851 Great Exhibition and the magnificent Crystal Palace (not designed by an architect but by gardener and engineer Joseph Paxton). Three strands of thought and approach emerged during the period under consideration.

First was the Arts and Crafts movement. This owes much to John Ruskin and later, William Morris, a man of the arts and a socialist. He was appalled by the poor quality of objects produced by the mid-Victorian industrial system, which also condemned workers to a life of misery and human degradation. He had a vision of a more satisfying and rewarding life in the Middle Ages when men were happy and creative working with their hands, rather than tediously tending machines in a dreadful Victorian factory. Morris also admired the architecture of the Middle Ages, inspiring his architect friends to revive such designs, albeit stripped of ornament and decoration. In Leeds three buildings reflect this approach. The Hostel of the Resurrection, 1907–10, is late Medieval/Tudor in style, modelled on an Oxbridge college in brick with stone dressings. However, its historic guise conceals an internal steel and concrete structure. The Roman Catholic cathedral of St Anne, 1902–4, is in stone, and both buildings have crenellated parapets in the medieval manner. In Headingley, South Parade Baptist church displays similar Arts and Crafts influences.

Oxford Place Methodist Centre, Oxford Place (1903). The original chapel in a simple Georgian style was built in 1835 by James Simpson (this can be seen on the western façade). It was remodelled in the early twentieth century by W.H. Thorp and G.F. Danby.

Arts and Crafts philosophies also renewed interest in traditional vernacular buildings. Architects influenced and inspired by William Morris and Co. produced houses that respected local craftsmanship and natural materials. Simplicity without ornamentation was the keynote with unadorned surfaces, horizontal fenestration and emphasis. Richard Norman Shaw and Charles Voysey were national figures who no doubt influenced local architects Bedford and Kitson, who designed many Leeds buildings at the turn of the century. Lincombe, 1898, and Red Hill, 1901, are houses in Headingley that are modest in size and simple in design. Similar designs are to be seen in the garden cities and suburbs of Letchworth, Port Sunlight and New Earswick, York (for Joseph Rowntree).

R.N. Shaw also introduced the Queen Anne Revival or Renaissance style, firstly in London, 1877. Here red brick walls, tiled roofs and dormers and white sash windows were featured in a simple manner. The former City of Leeds Training College at Beckett Park, 1911, and former Public Dispensary, 1904, in North Street, Leeds, are typical local examples. This design approach continued into the twentieth century, particularly for public and official buildings.

The second strand of approach is that of Art Nouveau. Sometimes described as the Style 1900, it originated in Belgium and France from

Entrance sculpture, Centenary House, North Street (1904).

Right: Grand Arcade, New Briggate (1897), designed by Smith and Tweedale.

Below: Leeds city markets – statuary, Vicar Lane (1904).
Below right: Armley Public Library, Stocks Hill (1901), designed by Percy Robinson.

around 1895. It was essentially a decorative two-dimensional surface treatment giving rise to slender, sinuous, undulating and asymmetrical forms. Typical subjects included natural plant forms, flames, flowing hair and the female form. In City Square, Leeds, the 'Morn' and 'Even' sculptures, 1903, are typical of the style. The entrance to Armley Branch Library, 1901, has features of natural forms. Terracotta and glazed ceramics were ideal mediums for displaying Art Nouveau designs and several Leeds buildings have examples on their façades, including the Chambers at 10–11 East Parade, 1899, with inventive lettering above the entrance. The figure of Atlas in Marmo terracotta looks down from above the door of Atlas House, King Street, 1910. Nearby, the Metropole Hotel, 1899, has a façade richly decorated with Art Nouveau style features.

Two major buildings in Vicar Lane include elements of the Art Nouveau as part of 'mixed' styles. The County Arcade (now Victoria Quarter), 1897–1902, is mainly Jacobean in style with a wide variety of rich and colourful materials, including marbles, mosaics, gilded features and elaborate ironwork. The City Market, 1904, is faced in stone with an elaborate roofline of dormers and spires inspired by the architecture of continental Europe. The entrance arches have spandrels of carved Art

Above: Statuary in City Square (1903): one of eight statues supporting lamps (not original). Four of the lamps are described as 'Morn' and four as 'Even'.

East Parade Chambers, 10–11 East Parade (1899): interesting lettering and mouldings in terracotta.

Top: Atlas House, sculpture, 31 King Street (1910), designed by Perkin and Bulmer. *Above:* Leeds Estates Company Development, between Briggate and Vicar Lane (1897–1902). This design by Frank Matcham included two arcades, two new streets, a theatre, shops and restaurants. It is now known as the Victoria Quarter.

Nouveau decorations and (modern) lettering and ironwork in a similar style. Art Nouveau could never have formed the basis of new architecture, being essentially superficial, a surface decoration not fully integrated with function, construction and structure.

The third influence on the buildings of this period was technically based on the use of 'new' materials and techniques. Sheet glass, cast and wrought iron and steel had been used to create huge bridges and massive buildings during the latter part of the nineteenth century. Following designs by engineers, some very large spaces were enclosed, forming railway termini, plant houses (as at Kew Gardens) and market halls. In Leeds the Corn Exchange roof and dome are a good example of such technology. The use of steel framing for buildings was introduced in Chicago, USA, in the 1870s after the Great Fire. This had the effect of reducing the mass and weight associated with traditional buildings with their load-bearing walls. Larger areas of windows could be introduced and internal layouts and spaces could be more flexible. Overall, the appearance

The former Empire Palace Theatre, Briggate. On the right of the picture, the theatre is the only part of the large development that has been lost by demolition and redevelopment. The site is now the Harvey Nicholls shopping development.

The County Arcade: a principal feature of the Matcham scheme. This view is from about 1907.

The County Arcade: restoration in 1990s. A comprehensive restoration and redevelopment scheme was undertaken late last century. This is a view of the restored ironwork, terracotta and lighting pendants.

Right: Leeds city markets, Vicar Lane (1904), designed by Leeming and Leeming and restored in the late twentieth century. *Far right:* Ironwork detail: the Civic Crest set within brackets to the structure. *Below*: Interior view from the early twentieth century. The clock was moved to Oakwood in 1912.

Hyde Park Cinema, Brudenell Road
(*c.* 1914). This represents a new type of
building for the new century, though this
is believed to have been converted from a
hotel.

Below: Bramley Baths, Broad Lane (1904).
The only survivor of eight public baths
built at the turn of the twentieth century,
this was recently restored preserving
original features.

of such buildings could be quite different, though many steel structures were still clad with 'historic' façades. The former Leeds College of Art, 1902, has huge studio windows on its north façade with exposed steel beams above. A former warehouse, 1903, on Wellington Street (now Apsley House) has large 'bay' windows similar to those to be seen on early Chicago skyscrapers.

Apsley House, 78 Wellington Street (1903). Originally a warehouse designed by George Corson and W.E. Jones with Perkin and Bulmer for Crowe and Co., this is now in office use.

Right: Leeds College of Art, Vernon Street (1903), designed by Bedford and Kitson.

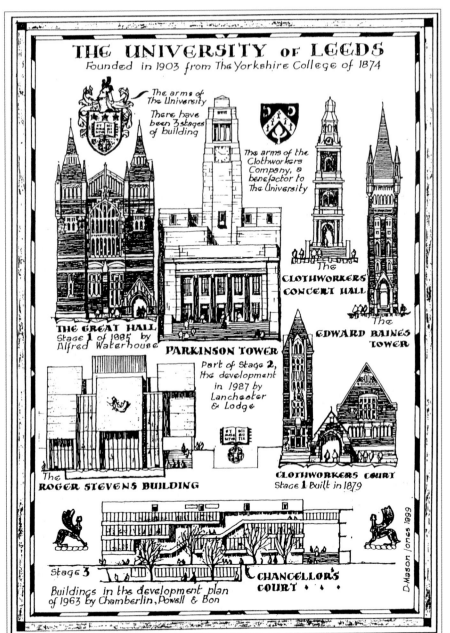

The University of Leeds through the years. This review of the changing face of the university over about eighty years is illustrated by these fine drawings by Denis Mason Jones. They follow the development from Victorian 'red brick', through mid-wars Portland stone to the ferro-concrete of the 1960s.

12   Twentieth-Century Leeds

The new 'international' or 'modern' styles were eventually to dominate the architectural scene after around 1950 but were received with considerable hostility in 'conservative' Britain between the wars. The work of architects Le Corbusier and Walter Gropius in continental Europe, with its crisp clean line images and functional theories inspired younger architects. However, most of the profession (and its clients) preferred to 'play safe' and used 'diluted' historic styles such as Arts and Crafts or simplified neo-Georgian.

Public buildings of the 1920s and 1930s tended to follow the latter principles. For instance, the Civic Hall, the Queens Hotel and the university are all based on simplified Classical styles, though, while being faced with Portland stone, they have steel frames and reinforced concrete floors. Apart from a few private houses, the only major Leeds buildings in the true modern style were the Quarry Hill Flats scheme. Built in the 1930s, their construction forecast the advanced building techniques that were developed and refined postwar. The flats were demolished in 1978 mainly because of technical problems, but much was learned from the failures.

Today economy is most important for efficient building. The production of machine-made components off-site (and under cover) speeds up the overall process, with less time spent on site. Standardise, mass produce and prefabricate are phrases that would not have pleased the early Arts and Crafts pioneers. However, these processes were used to construct the Quarry Hill Flats and they are still widely employed today; one only has to think of the simple building brick to see that they are not new. Bricks have always been mass produced to a standard size and shape. Their design allows bonding with a unit twice as long as it is wide and their size and weight allows them to be picked up with one hand. Bricks have a long history.

The needs of today are very different from those of the past. There have been profound changes in lifestyles and we need many new and different types of buildings for industry, shopping, leisure and transport. The architecture of today has made a massive break with that of the past. Great strides have been made with the development of new materials and techniques. Once again necessity has proved to be the mother of invention.

MODERN IDEAS

The Arts and Crafts movement and the magnificent achievements of the Victorian engineers were to have a profound influence on the architecture of the twentieth century. While William Morris despised the use of the machine, the impact of his design philosophies, together with his enlightened thinking on social reform, found favour with many twentieth-century architects. The 'Modern Movement', the name given to the necessary re-evaluation of architecture and design early in the century, had its origins in the nineteenth-century works of pioneers Paxton, Shaw, Voysey, Lutyens and others.

Oakwood Fish Bar, 492 Roundhay Road (late 1930s). This Art Deco-style shopfront presents a strong visual contrast with its host building, a sober, stone Edwardian terrace.

Leeds Civic Hall, Calverley
Street (1933), designed by
E. Vincent Harris.

Leeds Civic Hall: a recent
view across Millennium
Square.

University of Leeds, Parkinson Building, Woodhouse Lane (completed 1951). This was designed in 1929–36 by Lanchester, Lucas and Lodge, together with the Brotherton Library and the Chemistry and Engineering Departments.

The Queens Hotel, City Square (1937), designed by W. Curtis Green and W.H. Hamlyn.

Increasingly, load-bearing steel and concrete structures were adopted for the construction of new buildings. These could now be higher with deep planning because of the use of electricity for lifts and lighting. As to the appearance of these buildings, architects have two choices. First the structural form can be exposed so that its use can be readily understood; in a sense, 'form follows function'. The second choice, taking a similar building, is to clad the structure with walls and features based on the historic past. The first approach flowered in continental Europe in the

1920s and 1930s, particularly in Germany and Holland, where new ideas were more readily accepted. Meanwhile, in 'conservative' Britain most larger public buildings were clothed in simplified period-style guises (mainly neo-classical) concealing the steel and concrete forms within.

In Leeds, very few Modern Movement buildings were erected prior to the 1960s, the only one listed being an Art Deco-style shopfront in Oakwood, Leeds, 1938. Several cinemas in this style were demolished in the postwar years. Several 1930s schools (unlisted) were built whose design was seemingly influenced by contemporary Dutch architecture, notably by W.M. Dudok at Hilversum.

Three major public buildings in Leeds are faced with smooth white Portland stone (from Dorset), a material alien to Leeds but fashionable for large government and commercial offices in London at the time. It was considered by city fathers that a fresh and clean appearance was needed for their new Civic Hall, 1933, so contrasting with the black and sooty streets around. The contrast must have come as quite a shock to citizens. The building's slender twin towers are reminiscent of Wren's London churches, unlike anything to be found in Leeds. Also in Portland stone, the Parkinson Building of the University of Leeds (designed 1929, completed 1951) presents a massive and grandiose neo-classical composition to Woodhouse Lane, its high white tower a well-known landmark. The third major building faced with Portland stone is the Queens Hotel, City Square, 1937. Again in a neo-classical style, it has a hint of Greek Revival with small temple-like features on the roofline. As the principal railway hotel (LMSR), it has the

Leeds City station concourse, City Square (*c*. 1935). Adjacent to the Queens Hotel, this is part of the original group of hotel and offices for the London, Midland and Scottish Railways.

main entrance to the concourse on its frontage. This was built in 1935 and
is a high wide space spanned by steel beams in a portal form. Its spacious
volume presents a very impressive introduction to the 'train sheds' beyond.

The Headrow was created in the early 1930s, the north side being
completely rebuilt after highway widening. The concept was to create a
grand thoroughfare similar to London's Regent Street. This model of early
town planning was built to a master plan by Sir Reginald Blomfield, and
parts of the long Headrow frontage, together with the Cookridge Street
building of the former Leeds Permanent Building Society, have been listed.
Again in neo-classical style, and also using Portland stone in conjunction
with red brick, the western section of this scheme now provides major parts
of The Light, a recent commercial development carefully integrated with
the existing 1930s buildings.

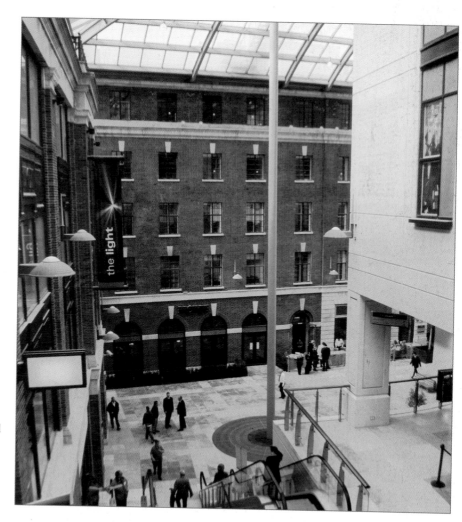

The Light, The
Headrow and
Cookridge Street
(2000). This
recent commercial
development
integrated with
and included the
1930s Headrow
scheme.

Northern School of Contemporary Dance, Chapeltown Road (1929–32). Formerly the United Hebrew Synagogue (closed in 1985), this was designed by J. Stanley Wright.

Church of the Epiphany, Gipton, Beech Lane (1938), designed by N.F. Cachemaille-Day.

Three original and individualistic places of worship are to be found in the north and eastern suburbs of Leeds. The former United Hebrew Synagogue, 1929–32, on Chapeltown Road is in a Byzantine style with a large copper dome. It is now a dance academy. Secondly the Church of the Epiphany, 1938, at Gipton is unique in that it is the only 'modern' building in Leeds to be protected by Grade One listing. Externally it has a solid fortress-like massing in brick, its curved and flat façades punctuated by very tall and narrow slit windows. Internally the main structure is of exposed reinforced concrete with 60-foot-high slender circular columns soaring up to flat ceilings. The whole is painted white, giving a light airy feel. The raised Lady Chapel in the east end apse is a more intimate space, its slit windows with fine glass depicting the Epiphany Stars. The church may not appear very inviting from the outside but internally its strong vertical emphasis alludes to Gothic historicism, but without decoration and ornamentation. A very unusual and original design.

The third church is only two miles from the Epiphany, in Halton. The Church of St Wilfrid, 1937–9, is another remarkable building. Architect Randall Wells had earlier worked with leading exponents of the Arts and

Church of the Epiphany, Gipton: the chapel in the east end apse.

Church of St Wilfrid, Halton, Selby Road (1937–9), designed by A. Randall Wells.

Church of
St Wilfrid, Halton,
Selby Road (1939),
designed by
A. Randall Wells.

The interior of the
Church of
St Wilfrid, Halton.

Crafts Movement. The church has a very original design whose massing is
again fortress-like, with groups of simplified angular lancet windows set
within pointed arches flush with the stone walling. The flat roofs are
concealed by parapets capped with stones set on edge, in the manner of a
Yorkshire field wall. The crossing is marked by a complex timber-faced 'spire'
with a Scandinavian feel. Internally the space is light and airy, with white
'vaults' in a strongly painted arched form, an approach probably influenced
by contemporary German church designs. Like the Epiphany, St Wilfrid's is
also highly rated, its original qualities attracting Grade 2* listed status.

13   Curiosities

Have you ever seen something that you have found surprising or puzzling because it looks odd, or at least unusual? Perhaps we are conditioned by living and working in a largely standardised environment of suburban housing estates, open plan offices or bland factory estates.

Here and there can be found individual and eccentric features of earlier generations, reminders of the way they lived, worked and died. Evidence of industries long gone, former country house estates and follies, a visit by a monarch and, for good measure, a zoo, and, shades of Biggles, a Royal Flying Corps hangar from the First World War! All are to be found within the Leeds Metropolitan District and all are listed, primarily for historical reasons.

Former aircraft hangar, Spen Common, Bramham (1916). An unusual survivor from the former Bramham Moor Airfield, which was the home of 33 Squadron of the Royal Flying Corps in 1916. The Squadron was part of the air defences of Leeds and Sheffield. The airfield was sold in 1919, but the hangar remained, in agricultural use. The drawing depicts how the airfield might have looked during its operational days. The building is of timber construction with Belfast roof trusses.

Civic fountain, Quarry Hill, Eastgate. A former petrol station (above), this was designed as a focal point of The Headrow redevelopment scheme by Sir Reginald Blomfield (1932). Having been listed, it was retained and remodelled as an illuminated fountain feature in 1999 (left). In the background of the earlier photo can be seen the former Quarry Hill Flats (demolished in 1979).

Contrasting reminders of the past.
Above: The remains of Boston Lodge, Boston Road,
Wetherby. This was originally part of the
nineteenth-century Wetherby Grange Estate.
The site is now used for police station and
magistrates' courts, which are screened from the
busy A1 by this feature.

Right: Truck-lifting tower, Aireside Centre,
Wellington Street. Not the remains of the Leeds
Castle Keep! Built in 1847, this is a surviving
remnant of the large Great Northern Railway
complex (originally there were two). Trucks could
be transferred from the low-level goods station to
the high-level passenger lines above.

Above: Gipton Well, Gledhow Valley Road. A spa in Leeds! The Waddington Bath was open to the air and 10 ft square, enclosed by high stone walls adjacent to a small bath house. Dated 1671 but rebuilt in the eighteenth century, it was well frequented. Visitors included Leeds historian Ralph Thoresby and Lord Irwin of Templenewsam.

Gazebo at Bramhope. Perhaps more accurately a belvedere, it is in a suburban garden overlooking a magnificent vista across Wharfedale towards Great Alms Cliff. Elegant proportions in sandstone with domed roof. A survivor from the now demolished Bramhope Hall.

Battlements in North Leeds!
The Old Castle, Roundhay
Park. This sham ruined
castle folly was built for
Thomas Nicholson in 1821
and is set at the head of
Waterloo Lake.
The Nicholsons used the
castle as a summer house
and sewing rooms for their
daughters.

Above: The Old Bear Pit, Cardigan Road,
Headingley. Leeds Zoological and Botanical
Gardens opened in 1840 but closed in 1858,
having had three owners. The only building that
survived is the Bear Pit, where the animals could
be viewed from above in the circular stone
towers. *Above, right:* Alma Cottages, off
Headingley Lane. They were originally privies for
these tiny cottages, built in about 1860, but are
now in use as storage and potting sheds. The
crenellated parapets and decorative window
heads and surrounds add distinction to this
humble building.

Victoria Arch, in Queen's Wood, Beckett Park.
The stone arch feature was probably erected in
Queen's Wood in the late eighteenth century.
The Beckett family bought the estate (then
known as Kirkstall Grange) in 1834 and William
Beckett added the tiled inscription in 1858 when
the Queen opened Leeds Town Hall.

14   *The Future*

We have seen how the architecture of today has made a break with the recent past. The slow evolution of our buildings over the centuries has taken major strides forward during the past few decades in line with all the arts, sciences and humanities. Contemporary architecture reflects these and is the expression of them all, whether it be a modern hospital, sports centre or shopping complex.

The post-1945 period witnessed new experiments and approaches in architectural design. Innovative techniques, advanced technology and newly developed materials arrived on the scene. Several hundred buildings are now listed from this period, though none has been so designated within the Leeds district. The 1951 Festival of Britain Exhibition looked anew at the values and styles that were possible after a long period of wartime austerity. The architects aspired to designs with Scandinavian ideals and democracy reflecting Britain's emerging social welfare state.

The Macmillan years, 1957–63, were to see the radical transformation of our towns and cities as never before (or since). His famous utterance 'you've never had it so good' today seems at odds with the urban legacy. Decaying substandard housing, the loss of many fine buildings and the wholesale destruction of the cherished local scene were the order of the day. Massive construction programmes required the use of standardised prefabricated systems to achieve high numbers of housing completions. It is regrettable that so many of these failed technically or are now deemed unacceptable by today's users.

The conservation movement grew in strength in the 1980s, redressing to a degree the mistakes of the post-war period. Leeds was not unduly affected by enemy bombing and did not rush into early redevelopment like its neighbour Bradford. The city centre retained much of its historic core, which has been carefully protected and enhanced. The value of 'context' has been recognised, with new buildings designed so as to fit sensitively into the urban fabric. There is an increased public awareness of design matters today, with national and local award schemes and good media coverage.

There is no reason why the plural and varied approaches to architecture will not continue into the future, fulfilling whatever needs or site considerations are required. A belief in the possibilities of modern architecture is not incompatible with respect and admiration for the past. The qualities of good design are unchanging. To build frankly for our own time is the only honest way of maintaining our fine architectural traditions and rich historic heritage.

NOW FOR SOMETHING DIFFERENT!

So far I have presented a personal selection of those buildings regarded by others as important architecturally and/or historically. However, I do have some favourites, which may or may not find favour with the experts when it comes to protecting them by adding them to the statutory lists in the future.

Collingham Memorial Hall (1920), designed by W. Alban Jones in the Arts and Crafts tradition.

I have always been fascinated by the period between the end of the nineteenth century and the outbreak of the Second World War – a period of transition, as outlined in 'A Break with the Past', a melting pot of architectural thought and theory, ranging from cosy Arts and Crafts to the 'modernist' approach of Dutch and German pioneers. The former is represented by Collingham Village Hall, a charming example in stone and render, the latter by the former Quarry Hill Flats, that magnificent failure, overtaken by changing times and inadequate technology.

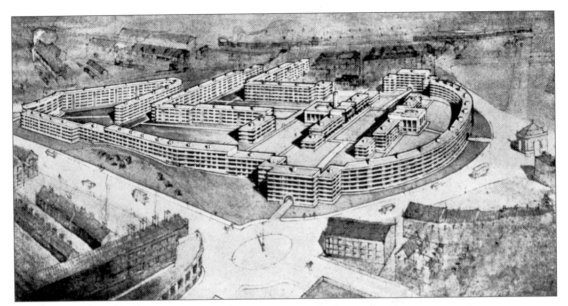

Above: The former Quarry Hill Flats, St Peter's Street (1936–79). They were designed by R.A.H. Livett, the Leeds City architect. With over 900 flats, the scheme was a pioneering development in the modernist functional style. The Headrow leads from the former petrol station on the extreme right of this drawing.

Allders Department Store, Bridge Road, Kirkstall (*c.* 1937). It was formerly a warehouse and offices for Thrift Stores.

Some of the best 1930s buildings in brick are in the Low Countries, notably in Hilversum by Willem Dudok, the municipal architect. The Town Hall is well known, a superb essay in cream brickwork. There are a few buildings in Leeds where brick has been used in a similar way. The design of the Allders Store in Kirkstall with its strong horizontal lines and contrasting clock tower was perhaps influenced by contemporary Dutch architecture. Two Leeds office buildings of the 1930s, Circle House off Eastgate, and Coronet House in Queen Street, are unassertive structures in brick, but good 'street architecture'. The former has a large and impressive glazed corner window wall lighting the stairwell. In the Leeds suburbs

St Augustine's Church, Harehills Road (*c.* 1938).

the Roman Catholic church of St Augustine, Harehills Road, has long been a favourite. Beautifully detailed in brick throughout, its entrance is particularly attractive and there is a strong consistency of design approach providing unified and satisfying architecture.

The Art Deco style, fashionable between the world wars, unfortunately offers few intact local examples. The fine curtain wall of the former Matthias Robinsons Department Store, Briggate (now Debenhams), has echoes of the style, with its steel windows and iron panels decorated with the typical chevron 'zigzag' patterns. However, these features are the only surviving part of the original building, 'gutted' in the late 1990s. Another building in the Art Deco style is in North Street, Leeds, originally in commercial use but now converted into apartments above the

Good 'street architecture'? Two office buildings.
Above: Coronet House, Queen Street (*c.* 1936).
Right: Circle House, Bridge Street (*c.* 1938).

Above: Debenhams department store, Briggate
(*c.* 1937).
Right: Showroom and apartments, 80 North Street
(*c.* 1936).

street level showrooms. In brick and cream faience, it has ironwork
window spandrel panels; the entrance archway and parapets are
particularly interesting. It is a pity about the recently added 'penthouse'
though, in a 'portakabin' style!

What of the last fifty years? I find it rather difficult to nominate examples
of this period that appeal to me. I feel that Leeds, despite its current
booming economy, has missed the boat in attracting the best in
contemporary architecture, those landmark buildings of national
significance. We rejected the 'Brick Man', but his winged brother the 'Angel
of the North' seems to be boosting Tyneside's fortunes. And Manchester
and Salford have the Lowry Centre, Imperial War Museum and
Commonwealth Games Stadium. Hull has the striking 'submarium', The
Deep (perhaps our Royal Armouries was a missed opportunity?). The only
Leeds building in the top category is the crystal-like fully glazed Princes
Exchange, by City station. A worthy winner of a City of Leeds Design
Award, the unusual structure is a direct response to the restricted site and
location next to the river. A more conservative and sober design produced
the Lloyds TSB building (Park Row), but there is great quality in detailing
and materials.

Opposite: Prince's
Exchange, off Aire
Street (1998)
(adjacent to the
City station
entrance).

Opposite: Two educational buildings with contrasting structures.
Top: The University of Leeds, Woodhouse Lane (*c.* 1960). It was constructed in exposed reinforced concrete and designed by Chamberlin, Powell and Bon.

Lloyds TSB, Park Row (*c.* 1979).

Above: Thomas Danby College, Roundhay Road (*c.* 1979). It was designed by the Leeds City architect, with exposed steel-framed structure.

One of the largest postwar developments in the city was the 1960s expansion of the University of Leeds. For the first time in Leeds, 'raw' *in situ* exposed concrete was used throughout in a consistent manner, though it has recently been painted. In contrast to the original buildings fringing the campus, a network of linked structures enclose urban scale courts and spaces. It is monumental in many ways, with dramatic views and vistas within, and out of, the campus. The central lecture theatre block and huge

flights of concrete stairs are sculptural elements within a robust urban setting, though recent landscaping has somewhat softened this quality.

Finally, what about the most numerous and famous (or should it be infamous?) of Leeds building types, the back-to-back house? I recall a student lecture in the 1950s when a city planner told us that all back-to-backs would be gone over the next twenty-five years! Will we ever get down to the last remaining terrace, preserving it for future generations? The National Trust is doing just that, in Birmingham. I have a particular and personal interest in this. I was born in the middle one in the photograph!

Back-to-back bye-law housing, Kepler Terrace (*c*. 1895). These houses are typical of many built in Leeds, the last back-to-back being erected as late as 1935. They have been upgraded to provide inside sanitation, better ventilation and improved kitchen facilities.

BIBLIOGRAPHY

Listed Buildings in Leeds, Department of Planning, Leeds City Council.
   A complete schedule with gradings, addresses and map references.
Leeds Street Atlas, Department of Planning, Leeds City Council.
   Covering the whole of the district.
Historic Buildings in Leeds: Understanding Listing, English Heritage and Leeds
   City Council.
Lists of Buildings of Special Architectural or Historic Interest.
   One volume covering the pre-1974 County Borough and nine for the
   outer areas. Often described as 'green backs', they are available for
   reference in the Leeds Local History Library and some branch libraries.

FURTHER READING

Brears, P., *Leeds Waterfront Heritage Trail.*
Burt, S. and Grady, K., *The Illustrated History of Leeds.*
Dimes, F. and Mitchell, M., *The Building Stone Heritage of Leeds.*
Fraser, D. (ed.), *A History of Modern Leeds.*
Hopwood, W. and Casperson, F., *Meanwood.*
Jackson, R., *Guide to Leeds.*
Jordan, R., *Victorian Architecture.*
Linstrum, D., *Historic Architecture of Leeds.*
——, *West Yorkshire Architects and Architecture.*
Pevsner, N., *The Buildings of England – Yorkshire The West Riding.*

SOME PUBLICATIONS BY AND AVAILABLE FROM LEEDS CIVIC TRUST

Dyson, P. and Grady, K., *Blue Plaques of Leeds.*
Douglas, J., *Leeds Places of Worship Trail.*
Godward, B., *Leeds Heritage Trail.*
——, *Leeds Then and Now.*
Hall, M., *Leeds Statues Trail.*